Dylan

Dylan

STEVE MATTEO

FOREWORD BY JUDY COLLINS

MetroBooks

MetroBooks

An Imprint of Friedman/Fairfax Publishers

©1998 by Michael Friedman Publishing Group, Inc.

Library of Congress Cataloging-in-Publication Data

Matteo, Stephen.
  Dylan / Stephen Matteo.
    p.   cm.
  Includes bibliographical references, discography, and index.
  ISBN 1-56799-634-5
  1. Dylan, Bob, 1941-   . 2. Singers—United States—Biography.
  I. Title.
  ML420.D98M17   1998
  782.42162'0092—dc21   97-51265

Editor: Francine Hornberger
Art Director: Kevin Ullrich
Designer: Garrett Schuh
Photography Editors: Karen Barr and Valerie E. Kennedy
Production Manager: Ingrid Neimanis-McNamara

Color separations by HK Scanner Arts Int'l Ltd.
Printed in Hong Kong by Sing Cheong Printing Company Limited

10 9 8 7 6 5 4 3 2 1

For bulk purchases and special sales, please contact:
Friedman/Fairfax Publishers
Attention: Sales Department
15 West 26th Street
New York, NY 10010
212/685-6610 FAX 212/685-1307

Visit our website:
http://www.metrobooks.com

Acknowledgments

There were many people that made this book possible. Steve Slaybaugh of Michael Friedman Publishing Group started the ball rolling when he asked me if I would like to write a biography of Bob Dylan. Along the way, editors Francine Hornberger and Steve Ciabattoni, photo editor Valerie Kennedy, production manager Ingrid Neimanis-McNamara, and designer Garrett Schuh kept the ball in the air. In the final stages, editor Emily Zelner carried the ball to the end zone. Suggestions, corrections, observations, and advice on the manuscript came from many helpful friends, colleagues, and experts, who took time from their hectic schedules during the time it took to make this book come to life. Joe Fallon from sunny California took time from his busy television writing schedule to quickly correct mistakes of all kinds, verify facts, and be there for tea and sympathy. Pete Fornatale brought his vast music knowledge to this project, and working with him was a dream come true. Lisa Pulitzer, David Pesci, Cynthia Blair, and Robert Walsh were also helpful in shaping the manuscript. Legal advice and career direction were offered by many, but Doug Pulitzer, David Sibek, and John Ortenberg were there in the clinch.

Inspiration came from many sources, but a few individuals stand out. Thanks to my family (Mom, Dad, Gina), my wife's family, and various other friends and neighbors too numerous to mention. Special thanks to those who fall under the "What-a-Long-Strange-Trip-It's-Been" category: Al Boccio, Fred Migliore (and the entire staff of FM Odyssey), Charles Garland, Bob Kranes, John Weston, Mark Biggs, and William "Rusty" Rustad.

Thank you to those far away or occasionally off the radar screen who helped without always knowing it: Robert Norton, Bill Moriarity, Gene Kerr, Jane Hamburger, Susan Honeyford, Pete Townshend, Brian Lindgren, Bill Ervolino, Wayne Robins, Anthony DeCurtis, Rod Ross, Vin Scelsa, and Canio Pavone. To Judy Collins, special thanks for coming through. I would like to respectfully thank those who are gone, in particular Alan Tesman.

This book would never have been possible without the editing skills, unfathomable patience, understanding, encouragement, and unwavering love of my wife, Jayne.

Dedication

To my son, Christopher. May you stay forever young.

Contents

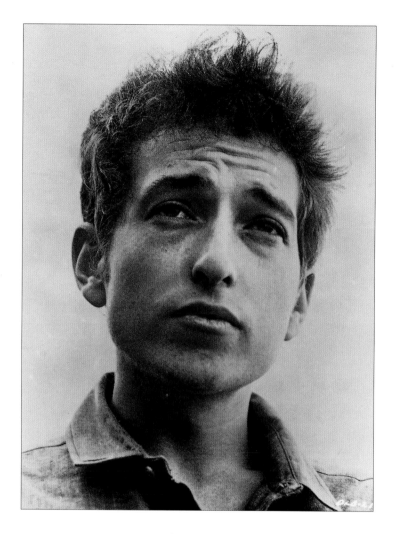

Foreword

The first time I met Dylan was at Gerdes Folk City. I remember getting drunk with him into the very late hours of the night and thinking that this guy, with his funky clothes—and you know, he was singing Woody Guthrie songs at that point—probably couldn't put two words together, let alone write a great song. Then I heard "Blowin' in the Wind" and changed my mind.

Parts of this book remind me of those days. We all wore these heavy boots back then, and it seemed like it was always snowing in New York. I remember wandering through the streets of Greenwich Village with Dylan and Susan, his girlfriend, and whistling and singing and catching snowflakes on our tongues—just being crazy kids.

Several years ago, I decided to explore all the Dylan songs that I didn't know by heart. I listened to almost everything that he ever recorded. It was a truly amazing experience to listen to Dylan straight through for a couple of weeks. It reminded me of why I am so passionate about this man's work: his writing is beautifully poetic and at the same time it is right on the cutting edge.

This is a wonderful book because it gives us a sense of the man, his writing, and his historical context. It shows us more of the mysterious, elusive Dylan we love but know so little about.

Judy Collins

Introduction

It's hard to convey in a mere biography the importance of Bob Dylan's place in popular music and the importance his music has had on the history and culture of the second half of the twentieth century. Dylan can easily stand alongside such other important figures of the century as Pablo Picasso, Jack Kerouac, and Charlie Chaplin. Not coincidentally, Dylan has crystallized the art of these three figures in his persona and in his approach to creating. Dylan himself, while no doubt an admirer of all three, always scoffs at his "importance." Any interviewer lucky enough to be able to interview him but naive, uninformed, or unimaginative enough to ask him how he feels about his place in music as such an important figure will be met with a roll of the eyes, a grunt, and a somewhat bored response. Dylan is reluctant to talk to the press, mistrusts the institution, and knows that many writers are more interested in the myth of Dylan and could never really know who he is. At first, it may appear to some that Dylan is a prickly, cranky character, but when one goes back over some of the interviews Dylan has had to endure over the years, it is a wonder he talks to the press at all.

Dylan's love-hate relationship with his audience and the media is essential to understanding who he is, or more accurately who we think he is. Being someone who has written about popular music for more than twenty years, I have always placed Dylan very far at the top of the list of artists I would want to interview. Knowing what I know about him, I have never even tried. I would love to interview Dylan for the same reason I would want to interview another subject equally mistrustful of the press and just as influential on the evolution of music in this century, Frank Sinatra: to learn. And not about the "good ol' days" or how a certain song was written, but to hear about the music these artists love and its history. It's very revealing reading Dylan's notes accompanying the 1997 album he organized, *The Songs of Jimmie Rodgers: A Tribute*, in which he says about Rodgers, "[He] was a blazing star whose sound was and remains the raw essence of individuality." These same words could be said about Dylan, yet he would be uncomfortable hearing them.

One can certainly empathize with Dylan's wanting to maintain any privacy he may have left after so many years as an icon. Like any father, he wants to keep his children safe from the glare of the media; yet one of his children, Jakob, of The Wallflowers, has now been thrust into the spotlight, and although he is not going through the same scrutiny his dad did, he instead may always be viewed as the son of Bob Dylan. Dylan's other children have also taken creative paths. Jesse is a video director; Sam is a photographer; and Anna is an artist. Maria, from Dylan's ex-wife Sara's previous marriage, however, is a lawyer and a mom.

Dylan still seems as restless as ever. He has lived in Woodstock; Greenwich Village; Phoenix, Arizona; Malibu; a farm in Laredo, Minnesota, not far from where he grew up; and the east end of Long Island; he has also traversed the seas in his boat. His touring pace could not likely be maintained by artists much younger. Nearing the age of sixty at this writing, Dylan shows no signs of slowing down. He seems to truly love the challenge of playing live. He also puts out albums that are not created with a marketing scheme in mind, but that are instead recorded as part of the evolution of his art. His late-1997 release, *Time Out of Mind*, makes it clear that he can still make truly great music.

Critics have pointed out that Dylan has raised the intelligence, sweep, and possibilities of pop songwriting; that he practically invented folk-rock and country rock; and that he was the archetype of the singer-songwriter—in 1998 Dylan won two Grammy Awards.

This biography is by no means all-inclusive. It merely traces Dylan's musical evolution up until late 1997. What I hope it accomplishes is to serve as an introduction to his works, a reconsideration of some of the periods of his art that have been completely misunderstood, and an appreciation of his dedication to being true to himself and his audience through his work. His story is also a wonderful account of how someone can rise up from even the most ordinary background and change the world. I strongly recommend that the reader further explore the other biographies and works about Dylan, his times, and other artists who have somehow been connected to him that are listed in the bibliography at the end of this book. I have always loved Dylan's music, have seen him perform many times, and have felt he was an important, if occasionally misunderstood, figure. The more I researched the Dylan story, the more I admired him. There have been so many times along the way when he could have retired from live performing and played the make-as-much-money-as-possible game, but he never has.

Mercurial, enigmatic, perplexing, occasionally anachronistic—in a good way, Dylan is a living legend, a man with a conscience, the musician's musician. This is the story of Bob Dylan's desire to make music. It is a portrait in miniature of a man who continues to live his life like a rolling stone, who for more than thirty years has hardly been a complete unknown, and who is still on the road with no direction home.

Steve Matteo

Opposite: *Dylan performing at Winterland in San Francisco at The Last Waltz concert, Thanksgiving 1976.*

CHAPTER ONE

Busy Being Born

Opposite: *Dylan at Gerdes Folk City, Manhattan, April 1961.* **Above:** *Robert Zimmerman's Hibbing High School yearbook photo, 1959. His ambition: to "join Little Richard."*

Bob Dylan's upbringing and home and community environments did not portend anything out of the ordinary. Bob Dylan was born Robert Allen Zimmerman on May 24, 1941, in Duluth, Minnesota. When he was six years old, his parents, Abraham and Beatty, moved to Hibbing, Minnesota, a timber and mining town where "Abe" became co-owner of a small appliance store. Bob had a brother, David, who was five years younger, and they had the kind of average suburban childhood that many postwar children had.

Although not born during the official baby boom years (1946–1964), Bob was shaped by the major cultural influences that affected all baby boom children, particularly rock and roll. Yet rock and roll shaped his attitudes primarily on the surface at first. The music that most influenced his teenage years also

included country, blues, R&B, and gospel. His musical education was facilitated by his ceaseless playing, both solo and with bands; scouring the racks at such local record shops as Crippa's; and meeting like-minded people who had big record collections that were usually filled with old, obscure country and blues. It was during his adolescence that he discovered old blues records, country artists, and the new rockers that shaped his sound. As Dylan told filmmaker and *Rolling Stone* reporter Cameron Crowe for the booklet that accompanied the 1985 *Biograph* box set, "I always wanted to be a guitar player and a singer. That was the only thing that I did that meant anything really." The first rocker who had any real early impact on Dylan, though, was piano player Little Richard, with his flamboyant, raucous, joyous style. The country artist who had the biggest influence on Bob's developing musical style and also impacted him lyrically was Hank Williams.

Rock and roll's influence on the American culture was transmitted to young Bob mostly through the idea that any young kid could form a band, which he did, one of the first being the Golden Chords. As Bob moved beyond just learning piano and guitar and writing poetry, he adopted the persona of James Dean, the defining role model for all aspiring teen rebel rockers of the 1950s. Part of this persona manifested itself in the purchase of a motorcycle at age fifteen. On the surface, Bob's attitude, clothing, motorcycle riding, and obsession with music may have appeared as just an adolescent "stage," but it was the foundation that began his journey from suburban kid to the voice of a generation to perhaps the single most important American rock figure of all time.

Somewhat of an outsider, young Bob was actually an average kid who by all accounts, beneath the rocker snarl, was often perceived as quite sweet. Because of his rather diminutive size and almost angelic countenance, he appeared harmless, which he was. He made the usual transition from high school kid to college student. This seemingly normal move, however, continued to shape his evolution as a musician and a person.

In the fall of 1959, Bob entered the University of Minnesota at St. Paul, where he had his first real taste of the bohemian life that helped define him for many years. "Minneapolis was the first big city I lived in, if you want to call it that," Dylan told Crowe for *Biograph*. "I came out of the wilderness and just naturally fell in with the beat scene, the bohemian....I had already decided that society, as it was, was pretty phony and I didn't want any part of that."

The university town, like many around the country in the late 1950s and early 1960s, had its little enclave of the emerging counterculture. The gathering place of prehippie bohemia in those days was the coffeehouse. Bob began his apprenticeship in the part of town known as Dinkytown, where budding

Above: Dylan in one of his earliest Greenwich Village performances at Folk City in April of 1961.

college radicals, hipsters, prototype hippies, punks, and slackers congregated. Often wearing the de rigueur black turtlenecks, jeans, and dark glasses, these young rebels would discuss politics, religion, poetry, and music until all hours of the morning, consuming espressos and cappuccinos to fuel their debates. It was here that Bob finally found a sympathetic stage for his early forays into professional or, more accurately, semiprofessional performing engagements. It was also around this time (although some accounts place it sooner) that Bob Zimmerman became Bob Dylan. Exactly when, why, and how this name change occurred are as shrouded in myth as anything he did to create the Dylan image, although most stories speculate that he took the surname of the television western character Matt Dillon and changed the spelling. The spelling change most likely came a bit later, and any borrowing from Dylan Thomas appears unfounded. Bob legally changed his name on August 9, 1962.

Dylan played at clubs such as the Ten O'Clock Scholar and the Purple Onion in St. Paul. It was at the Ten O'Clock Scholar that Dylan met and played with some of the musicians who, like himself, went on to become important musical artists in their own right. The first, John Koerner, became part of the blues trio of Koerner, Ray, and Glover.

Dylan was officially registered as a student for only three semesters. His real education came not from the books assigned in his classes, but from those suggested by fellow bohemians. Certain books had a profound influence on Dylan, an interest that went back to his high school days, when such John Steinbeck novels as *Cannery Row* and *The Grapes of Wrath* opened up whole other worlds to him. A fellow beatnik, David Whittaker, recommended a book that would be a defining experience in shaping the musical and spiritual persona of Bob Dylan: *Bound for Glory*, Woody Guthrie's autobiography. Guthrie was the original American troubadour of the twentieth century. His song "This Land Is Your Land" was as recognizable as the national anthem. Guthrie lived the life of a hobo, hopping freight trains and playing songs, and was perhaps the last true connection between the old cowboy and modern America. Here was a figure with whom the impressionable young musician could really identify. Dylan tried to learn every song Guthrie ever wrote or performed and did just about everything to adopt the look and the sound of his new hero, from Guthrie's dust-parched vocal groan to his worn work shirt.

Guthrie's influence had an effect on Dylan beyond his look, sound, and choice of material to perform. Dylan was so inspired by Guthrie and had such an affection for the man and his life that he wrote his first real song—"Song to Woody"—for Guthrie. Again, misconception and myth cloud the actual facts, but most likely Dylan wrote the song sometime during the trip he made on his first attempt to meet Guthrie when he stopped in Chicago on his way to New

Jersey, where Guthrie was staying. On the way, Dylan had another encounter with an artist who popped up again in Dylan's future and went on to a music career of his own: in Madison, Wisconsin, Dylan met and performed with Danny Kalb. Kalb was an extraordinary guitarist who was later part of a New York–based group called the Blues Project, whose keyboardist and leader, Al Kooper, became an important and longtime musical sideman for Dylan.

Before actually meeting Guthrie, Dylan made one last stop at the place that more than anywhere else on the map had the most musical and spiritual influence on his life: New York City—specifically, Greenwich Village. As Dylan told Crowe for *Biograph*, going to New York "was like going to the moon....You just didn't get on a plane and go there, you know....New York! Ed Sullivan, the New York Yankees, Broadway, Harlem—you might as well have

Above: *Woody Guthrie was the most profound influence on Dylan, and Guthrie's autobiography,* Bound For Glory, *was the blueprint for Dylan's early scuffling days.*

been talking about China. It was someplace [where] not too many people had ever gone, and anybody who did go never came back." Dylan arrived in Greenwich Village, the center of the folk scene, in January 1961 (although some accounts have him there earlier). With no more than the clothes on his back, a guitar, and a knapsack, Dylan began his slow ascent from a nobody to the most important folksinger ever.

It was also in New York where Dylan turned the art of creating the myth of Bob Dylan into a science. Rather than letting on that he was just some kid from suburban Minnesota who had spent the last few semesters at a midwestern college, Dylan told tales of hopping freight trains, living out west, and playing professionally with various musical artists from rock and roll and pop (including Bobby Vee, which actually almost took place in 1959), as well as with some of the greatest blues artists of all time. He also had the nerve to say that he had already played with his idol, Woody Guthrie, whom he actually came east to meet for the first time.

Dylan's stories showed him to be not so much an untrustworthy liar, but more emblematic of what many members of the baby boom generation were so adept at—re-creating and reinventing oneself as the person one wanted to be, moving beyond who one actually was or what the straight establishment expected one to be. Dylan's abilities to accomplish this and to do it with such ease and charm, even when people could easily figure out that his adopted persona wasn't true, were part of the twisted charm and magnetism that initially helped him gain the support of the Village regulars and launch his musical career.

In the 1960s, Greenwich Village was a veritable hothouse of musical and lifestyle expression and experimentation. Clubs such as the Commons, the Kettle of Fish, the Gaslight, and the Cafe Wha? were teeming with new and old folksingers, comedians, and performing artists of every stripe. With its narrow, tree-lined, cobblestone streets packed with coffeehouses, antique and thrift shops, and, above all, affordable rents and tolerant populace, the Village was again the home of the avant-garde as it had been in the early part of the century. An encouraging, freewheelin' sense of common bonhomie was just the place for Dylan to make his move. Ambitious, ambiguous, creative, and enigmatic, Dylan fit right in with the carnival-like cast of musicians, poets, writers, budding activists, and those simply searching for kicks, who made up the varied and rich tapestry of Village life.

Dylan naturally gravitated toward the center of the folk music movement: Izzy Young's Folklore Center and Mike Porco's Village folk nexus, Gerdes Folk City. Folk City was a hotbed of the folk movement, as were the Gate of Horn in Chicago, the Tin Angel in Philadelphia, and especially Club 47 in

Right: *Greenwich Village in the 1960s was the vortex of the folk scene and the hip place to be.*

Cambridge, Massachusetts. At the time of Dylan's arrival, Gerdes was the home of such folk and blues legends as Dave Van Ronk and Ramblin' Jack Elliott and such newcomers as Judy Collins and Tom Paxton. Elliott was an important figure to Dylan. Elliott had traversed the country with Guthrie, hopping freights and playing music, and he became the first true musical and spiritual heir of the Guthrie tradition. Also, like Dylan, Elliott created a persona of the singing hobo cowboy, although he came from an upper-middle-class family from, of all places, Brooklyn, New York.

Dylan became friendly with Van Ronk and Elliott, who were quick to appreciate his obvious respect for the great folk and blues tradition, yet also recognized that there was something very special and new about Dylan. His obviously less than truthful yarn spinning didn't cause Elliott and others to feel any less affection for him. They took him into their homes, since Dylan had nowhere to stay, and provided one of the links to Dylan's being so quickly accepted into Guthrie's circle.

In 1951 Guthrie started to suffer terribly from Huntington's disease, a degenerative illness that took his mother's life, and in 1954 he entered Brooklyn State Hospital. In 1959 he was committed to the Greystone State Hospital in New Jersey, where his friends would visit him. On weekends he would be taken to East Orange, New Jersey, to the home of Bob Gleason and his wife, Sid. Friends such as Elliott, Pete Seeger, and Cisco Houston (a traveling companion of Guthrie's who was also quite ill and close to dying) would get together to play music and help make Guthrie's difficult illness as bearable as possible. Dylan eventually found his way to these Sunday gatherings. According to various interviews over the years with those who were there, Dylan at first just sat quietly at his hero's feet, but eventually he sang his "Song to Woody" for the aging hobo. Woody immediately took to the aspiring folksinger, and would ask his friends if the young "boy" would be coming to visit again soon.

At this time, many of Dylan's Hibbing and Dinkytown dreams were coming true. He had done some traveling, had met Guthrie as well as other legends of folk and blues, and was living in Greenwich Village. He was starting to be recognized as someone to keep an eye on as a major new voice. With his Guthrie sound and look, and borrowing liberally from Elliott's arrangements of folk and blues songs as well as going so far as to adopt many of Elliott's stage mannerisms, he performed solo and with artists such as Fred Neil.

Dylan's biggest musical break came in April 1961, when he became the opening act on a two-week engagement of blues legend John Lee Hooker at Gerdes. For Dylan, as for other future giants like Bill Cosby, the Village clubs provided an important stage. The growing acceptance by and encouragement of his fellow folkies gave Dylan the confidence to begin performing his own

Left: *Dylan at The Bitter End, 1961.*

compositions, including such early talking blues songs as "Talkin' Bear Mountain Picnic Massacre Blues" and "Talkin' New York," in addition to the covers he played.

As fast as things were happening for Dylan, there were some setbacks. An appearance at the Cafe Lena in Saratoga, New York, in June 1961 did not go over very well, as many of those in attendance (and there weren't many) didn't quite get the Dylan thing. While his Village pals understood his odd stage antics (part Elliott and part Charlie Chaplin with, of course, generous helpings of Guthrie) and his anything-but-sweet vocal delivery, the Cafe Lena crowd was not moved.

Back in the Village, Dylan got a chance to get into a recording studio. He appeared on Harry Belafonte's *The Midnight Special* album playing harmonica on the title cut. The experience was not what Dylan expected. Usually performing fast and loose, with the rough edges left in, he felt out of place with Belafonte's slick professionalism and countless takes. Dylan's desire to work quickly in the studio affected his usual approach to recording, sometimes causing him frustration and at other times resulting in his recordings not being as good as they could be.

Getting into the studio proved to be an important turning point in Dylan's career. While the planning of a recording session for folksinger Carolyn

Above: *In the late 1950s, Greenwich Village (above) and San Francisco were the locales most supportive of the new poetry.*
Opposite: *John Hammond, Sr., right, signed Dylan and guided him through his early recordings.*

Hester was under way, Dylan, who was to perform on her album, met one of the two men who would be most responsible for bringing his music to a mass audience: John Hammond, Sr., the tall, erudite, avuncular figure who, along with Goddard Lieberson, made Columbia Records into a recording label that was both commercially successful and respected. Hammond was one of the top

THE FOLKLORE CENTER

Presents

BOB DYLAN

IN HIS FIRST NEW YORK CONCERT

·o·o·o·o·o·o·o·o·o·o·

SAT. NOV. 4, 1961   8:40pm

CARNEGIE CHAPTER HALL

154 WEST 57th STREET • NEW YORK CITY

All seats $2.00

Tickets available at: The Folklore Center
110 MacDougal Street
GR 7 - 5987   New York City 12, New York

honchos of Columbia Records. He brought Billie Holiday, Benny Goodman, Count Basie, and later Aretha Franklin and Bruce Springsteen to the label, and was considered by many to be one of the most important and knowledgeable record men around, whose chief skill was discovering new talent.

After further session work on recordings for Victoria Spivey and Big Joe Turner, two events helped Dylan gain entrance into the big time. In September 1961 he opened for the Greenbriar Boys at Folk City and received a glowing review in *The New York Times* by Robert Shelton that called Dylan the most important new voice in folk music. Reportedly at the same time, Dylan recorded some demos for Hammond and was quickly signed to the label. He then began the process of recording his debut album. (Conflicting reports indicate that Dylan never did any demos and that Hammond signed him based on Shelton's review; glowing praise from his son, blues artist John Hammond, Jr., and others; and a performance or two he attended.) After the Hester sessions, the excitement of securing a record deal delighted Dylan. "I couldn't believe it," he said in the *Biograph* notes. "I remember walking out of the studio. I was like on a cloud. It was up on Seventh Avenue and when I left I was happening to be walking by a record store. It was one of the most thrilling moments in my life. I couldn't believe that I was staring at all the records in the window...and soon I, myself, would be among them in the window."

Dylan was performing, writing songs, playing on other people's albums, and now recording his own album on one of the biggest record labels in the world. Everything was in place for a real musical "career," something Robert Zimmerman had always wanted, yet something that seemed anathema to what Bob Dylan stood for. Behind the scenes, the final piece of the puzzle to solidify Dylan's career was about to surface, unbeknownst to just about everyone.

Albert Grossman had opened the Gate of Horn club in Chicago, had coproduced the first Newport Folk Festival with George Wein in 1959, and was managing Odetta. Seeing the way folk music was becoming so popular with the emergence of a group like the Kingston Trio, he assembled Peter, Paul and Mary and got them signed to Warner Brothers Records. For all of Grossman's perceptiveness and apparent love for the music, his persona was another thing altogether. He was a big, imposing man with an intimidating demeanor who looked like a hip Ben Franklin. His apparent cunning, business smarts, and lack of fear of confronting anyone who didn't have his artists' best interest in mind made him a formidable manager. Again, the story of the life and career of Bob Dylan includes many holes in terms of exactly how Dylan and Grossman met and decided to strike an agreement. What is clear is that Grossman, for all his high-pressure, slick management style, had the foresight to recognize the commercial promise that Dylan had. Many in the Village and at Columbia were very unsure whether Dylan's rough style could be understood and marketed beyond the Village denizens who appreciated the uniqueness of his musical and personal charms.

The recording of Dylan's first album marked the beginning of his run-ins with those artists who felt that perhaps his ascent had happened too quickly. There were many people in the Village scene who had played and struggled for years yet could not secure a big recording contract with a powerhouse like Columbia. However, there were many musicians who were thrilled that one of their own had gone beyond the old folk sound and created something new. For some time, many people in the Village crowd, particularly Dave Van Ronk, had pushed Dylan to move past the Guthrie- and Seeger-inspired songs that said more about the 1930s than the 1960s. While the songs he recorded for his first album didn't create anything dramatically new, the foundation was in place. By the time that first album was released, many outside and personal events had inspired Dylan to create songs that would revolutionize the folk song vocabulary and style beyond Van Ronk's, Dylan's, or anyone's wildest dreams. In a short time, Bob Dylan almost single-handedly ushered in the sociopolitical explosion of the 1960s. And he was its leading proponent for several years.

Above: *This poster announced Dylan's first official New York performance.* **Opposite:** *Dylan recording his debut album in Manhattan, 1962.*

CHAPTER TWO

Son of Woody

Opposite: *Recording in 1962 at Columbia studios.* **Above:** *Dylan, his guitar, and his harmonica in 1963.*

voice for that genre, the average record-buying public at that time was sending other kinds of music to the top of the charts. Though rock and roll had been losing its early luster for some time, there were still plenty of hits from the likes of Sam Cooke and Joey Dee & the Starlighters, and Tamla/Motown was placing high on the charts with such hits as the Marvelettes' "Twistin' Postman." Music lovers were more interested in twisting, which was the latest dance craze: there were at least five songs with the word "twist" in them on the charts. There was also a continuing emergence of middle-of-the-road singers who were more pop than rock that winter, including Patti Page, Connie Francis, Bobby Rydell, Paul Anka, Bobby Vee, and even Shelley Fabares. The Kingston Trio had "Where Have All the Flowers Gone" and the Everly Brothers were bringing a sophistication to music with their harmonic blend of country, pop, and rock in "Crying in the Rain," but in general, the climate was not exactly ripe for Dylan's recording debut.

The talk of Dylan being dropped continued at Columbia, with some dubbing Hammond's signing of Dylan as "Hammond's Folly." Along with the fact that Columbia had had most of its success with very middle-of-the-road pop music, there probably were many people at the label who just plain didn't understand Dylan or his potential, or were jealous of Hammond's success over the years of spotting talent and signing some of Columbia's most important artists. That the debut contained only two original compositions ("Talkin' New York" and "Song to Woody") perhaps contributed to the album's relative lack of sales, since as new as Dylan was to many, the cover songs on the album were only competent reworkings of folk, blues, and traditional songs.

In the aftermath of his less-than-earth-shattering debut, personal and external forces drove Dylan to begin writing the first of his songs that were truly original in sound and reflected, more eloquently than any folk- or rock song had ever done, the inner and political struggles that shaped the generation. In October 1962, the United States was gripped with fear regarding the Cuban missile crisis. With the United States and the Soviet Union teetering on the cusp of war, Dylan, having already written such clear-cut antiwar songs as "Blowin' in the Wind" (a big hit for Peter, Paul and Mary) and "Masters of War," penned "A Hard Rain's A-Gonna Fall." These songs were not songs of long-forgotten foreign wars, the Civil War, or some generic conflict; rather, they were about the current state of warfare, where the final result was potential nuclear annihilation. By writing these songs, Dylan had begun the process of defining the contemporary protest song. An example is the song "Blowin' in the Wind," about which in the *Biograph* notes Dylan remarked, "It was just another song...and got thrown into all the songs I was doing at the time. I wrote it in a cafe across the street from the Gaslight. Although I thought it was

Dylan's self-titled debut album was released in March 1962. It sold poorly, creating a growing feeling at Columbia that Dylan should be dropped. Many had hoped the album would have more of Dylan's own compositions. "I just took in what I had," Dylan recalled. "I tried a bunch of stuff and John Hammond would say, 'Well, let's use this one,' and I'd sing that one and he'd say, 'Let's use that one.' I must have played a whole lot of songs. He kept what he kept, you know. He didn't ask me what I wrote and what I didn't write. I was only doing a few of my own songs back then, anyway."

While his fellow folkies fully understood how Dylan was paying homage to the great folk and blues tradition and at the same time presenting a new

Above: *Dylan had an up-and-down relationship with folk song magazines such as* Broadside.

special, I didn't know to what degree; I wrote it for the moment, ya know." Like many of his early compositions, it was published in the folk song magazine *Broadside*. Like its predecessor and sometime friendly rival, *Sing Out!*, *Broadside* included the words and music of folk songs. Unlike *Sing Out!*, though, *Broadside* was interested in the topical protest songs that Joan Baez was singing, that Dylan was just starting to write, and that many others, like Phil Ochs, would later write and perform.

It was at this time that Dylan's personal life began affecting his songwriting as it never had before. He was involved in a serious relationship with Suze Rotolo. Dylan had had the requisite high school sweetheart, Echo Helstrom,

back in Minnesota, and a slew of other relationships of varying degrees of duration and intensity, but for both Suze and Bob, this was the kind that for the first time included living together and talk of marriage. The two, by all accounts, were very much in love, yet because of their age, intensity, and conflicting career paths (she was involved in various creative jobs, including theater scene design), they had the expected ups and downs. The relationship inspired Dylan to write love songs in addition to the topical protest songs at which he was becoming so proficient. When Suze went away on a trip to Italy with her family—something he did not want her to do—he wrote the pain-filled song "Don't Think Twice, It's All Right." The song was actually based on a melody

Above: *Dylan was an early supporter of civil rights and often gave benefit concerts to support the cause.*

from a song in the public domain called "Who'll Buy Your Chickens When I'm Gone," which was discovered by fellow Village folkie Paul Clayton.

Traveling to London, possibly in an attempt to be closer to Suze, he wrote two of his most beautiful early love songs, "Boots of Spanish Leather" and affectionately remembering his first love, Echo, "Girl from the North Country." It was also at this time that Dylan, about to be ordained the unofficial prince and future king of folk, wrote a song called "Mixed-Up Confusion," his first complete band session, which contains the earliest elements of a full-blown rock sound in one of his songs—a sound that in only a few short years would become the style he would adopt, abandoning the typical folk protest

song. The song was immediately withdrawn upon release because it was so different from Dylan's other work.

While Dylan was kicking around the Village, seeming lost to his friends after the poor reception of his debut album, and with Suze being very far away, Albert Grossman and his fellow folksingers were touting his genius across the country. Though it wouldn't become a full-fledged national hit until July 1963, "Blowin' in the Wind" was being covered by Peter, Paul and Mary, who made it clear during their performances that the song was written by a young man named Bob Dylan. And it was Peter, Paul and Mary's rendition of the song that made it a hit. With Grossman liberally stoking the fires of hype, Peter, Paul and Mary and other folksingers, during appearances on college campuses across the country, touted Dylan as the next "voice of a generation," expediting his rise to national stardom.

Just before Dylan released his second album, *The Freewheelin' Bob Dylan*, in 1963, Grossman secured him a spot on the highly influential Sunday night CBS variety program *The Ed Sullivan Show*. It was at this time that one of the first controversies in a lifetime of controversies for Dylan arose. Dylan wanted to perform the song "Talkin' John Birch Society Blues." CBS, fearing the wrath of the Society and of similarly sympathetic organizations and individuals, wouldn't let him sing the song. The ensuing flap prompted Columbia to initially pull the song from the about-to-be-released *Freewheelin'* album and resulted in three different albums under the same title being released, each with a slightly different track selection. And Dylan never appeared on the show.

Upon the May 1963 release of *The Freewheelin' Bob Dylan*, with John Hammond credited as producer (though many of the tracks were in fact produced by Tom Wilson), Dylan began a relationship with Joan Baez that would change over and over, publicly and privately, well into the 1980s. While they were at the Monterey Folk Festival they really got to know each other, and Dylan was a guest at Baez's home in Carmel, California. She had become the personification of the new folk movement—or, more accurately, the singing voice of it, since unlike Dylan she was not primarily a songwriter. Her pure, high soprano voice, dark looks, and political activism made her the queen of the new folk scene; she had even appeared on the cover of *Time* magazine in 1962 (which, oddly enough, she would lampoon on her album *Blowing Away* in 1977). Her presence, along with that of Peter, Paul and Mary, Theodore Bikel, and Pete Seeger, made the 1963 Newport Folk Festival the biggest ever. Baez spent much of her energy introducing and/or further championing Dylan at her concerts. She would usually play the first half of her show by herself, singing many of Dylan's songs that appeared on *Freewheelin'*; then she would bring Dylan out and the two would sing together. Finally, Dylan would sing alone.

Opposite: *Dylan with Suze Rotolo, one of his many girlfriends who was also his muse.*
Above: *Under the supervision of John Hammond, Sr., Dylan recorded his debut album in 1962.*

some sense of both the civil rights struggles and the growing antiwar movement of the day. Organizations like the NAACP and CORE were gaining momentum, and newer, more militant organizations like the Southern Christian Leadership Counsel—led by a young minister named Martin Luther King, Jr.—and the Student Non-Violent Coordinating Committee were speaking out, holding rallies, and raising their collective voices in rage over racial inequality in the United States. In June 1962, the organization Students for a Democratic Society (SDS), which had grown from a group of activist students at the University of Michigan at Ann Arbor (led by Tom Hayden, among others), put forth the Port Huron Statement, decrying everything from war to racial and economic inequality, commercialization, continuing corruption, and the rise of the military industrial complex. These organizations later gave rise to the Free Speech Movement, led by Mario Savio at the University of California at Berkeley, and similar political and social movements in other parts of the country. What these organizations lacked was a galvanizing force, a popular voice that would tie their anger, disillusionment, and righteous fury together to reach beyond a few select college campuses and coffeehouses.

In August 1963, the Reverend Martin Luther King, Jr., led a march on Washington, D.C., further solidifying the civil rights movement. The songs on *Freewheelin'* perfectly reflected this mood and collective cry for change. "Blowin' in the Wind" was the perfect call to end wars and gave new voice to the ban-the-bomb movement, which had begun in England and was sweeping progressive antiwar minds in the United States. By this time Peter, Paul and Mary's version of the song was a huge hit. Dylan's "A Hard Rain's A-Gonna Fall," originally written around the time of and inspired by the Cuban missile crisis, still resonated with anyone who suspected that the cold war could ignite into a nuclear apocalypse at any moment. "Masters of War" placed the blame for war squarely on the shoulders of the politicians and technocrats who fanned the flames of warfare for their own monetary and power gains. Dylan, in looking back on the song, said, "That's pretty self-explanatory, that song. But I never felt it was goodbye, or hello. I was just there. I was just in it, and if I wasn't, I wasn't. But I did what I could while I was there, you know, I don't know, in lots of ways I'm still there in some kind of way, not protest for protest's sake but always in the struggle for peoples' freedom, individual or otherwise. I hate oppression, especially on children."

"Oxford Town" fit perfectly into the broadside tradition, as it was inspired by the enrollment of James Meredith in the all-white University of Mississippi. Meredith's brave move was one of many events that brought the civil rights issue to the attention of the nation. In Greensboro, North Carolina, four black college students sat in the "whites only" section of the Woolworth's lunch counter and sparked a sit-in that eventually forced the four to be served. When

The effects of *Freewheelin'* on the music world made many forget how poorly Dylan's first album had performed. On the cover, Dylan and Suze are huddled closely together as they move down a Greenwich Village street on a cold winter day, both affectionately smiling. The cover seemed to capture the mood of the Village perfectly; the inside contained love songs as well as Dylan's seminal topical songs.

The year 1963 was pivotal for the social and political upheavals that defined the decade and influenced Dylan and countless other writers, singers, poets, filmmakers, and cultural and political figures who were beginning to shape the segment of the population just reaching young adulthood. After the Cuban missile crisis came other cultural, social, and political events that had an enormous effect on the new, college-educated, prosperous generation.

To truly understand the importance of Dylan's music at that time and his tremendous contribution to art, politics, culture, and society, one must have

Above: *Joan Baez and Dylan performing together in 1963.* **Opposite:** *Dylan in New York's Greenwich Village, the hothouse environment that nurtured him early on.*

four young girls were killed when a bomb went off in Birmingham, Alabama, even those who didn't pay much attention to the rising voice against racial inequality were outraged. Emerging from this vortex of rising consciousness, violence, rage, and bravery, Dylan's songs became the soundtrack of the many events and movements that came to define the tumultuous 1960s.

Toward the end of 1963, a cataclysmic event happened that further fueled the paranoia that was sweeping the young and began the violence that marked the decade: the assassination of President John F. Kennedy on November 22. The album *The Times They Are A-Changin'* was released a little more than a month later, in January 1964. It could not have been more fitting of the times. Very much a sequel to *Freewheelin'*, it further expressed the growing unease among the young about the world they were inheriting.

The Cuban missile crisis as well as the deaths of the young president and those killed in the name of civil rights, not to mention the growing awareness of the hypocrisy and injustice of the Vietnam War, shaped the themes of such songs on the album as "Ballad of Hollis Brown"; "With God on Our Side"; "Only a Pawn in Their Game," about the murder of Medgar Evers, the head of the NAACP; and the title track. The album's most chilling song, "Lonesome Death of Hattie Carroll," was written in a small restaurant on Seventh Avenue in Manhattan. Alluding to the song in the *Biograph* notes, Dylan said, "I felt I had a lot in common with the situation and was able to manifest my feelings. The song itself is about the death of a black woman in February 1963 at the hands of a socialite, whose father was able to get her off with a light sentence because he was heavily involved in Maryland politics. The set pattern to the song I think is based on [Bertolt] Brecht's 'The Ship, the Black Freighter.' " ("The Ship, the Black Freighter" is part of the lyrics of "Pirate Jenny" in *The Threepenny Opera*.) The album marked the end of an era for Dylan, both personally, and professionally. It was his last albumz to contain entirely folk and protest songs, and the beginning of a major stylistic change.

While all this was happening, Dylan's life was changing dramatically. With his growing popularity, his anointed sainthood as the folk troubadour of truth and justice, his relationship with Suze disintegrating while his relationship with Baez intensified, and his demanding touring and recording schedule, Dylan found the time he had to himself diminishing. The demands made on him by friends, Grossman, and Columbia would have been enough to drive anyone crazy. But Dylan continued to write songs and, thanks to Grossman, had access to a place where he could get some peace. This geographic locale not only had an enormous effect on Dylan and his music, but it was near another place that would become significant to millions of individuals of the counterculture as the decade ended. Grossman had a place in Bearsville, New York, not far from the artists' colony of Woodstock. It was in Bearsville that Dylan spent time relaxing, writing, and reading, free of the pressures of the Village and New York City.

Dylan's songs became even more complex as he read more poetry and literature, following in the footsteps of the San Francisco poetry renaissance known as "the beats." Symbolist poetry, mostly by Arthur Rimbaud, had a tremendous influence on Dylan's life and music. A song that resulted from his reading of Rimbaud was "Mr. Tambourine Man." Dylan explained that the song "was inspired by Bruce Langhorne....Bruce was playing guitar with me on a bunch of the early records....On one session, [producer] Tom Wilson had asked him to play tambourine. It was like really big. It was as big as a wagon wheel. He was playing, and this vision of him playing this tambourine just stuck in my mind."

Those were heady times for Dylan. He appeared as the headliner at a Carnegie Hall concert, which his parents attended; Dylan no longer felt the need to hide his past. In his early scuffling days he told people that he had no parents and created other stories to further the Dylan myth. Even with all the confusion, Dylan was now trying to get his life straight, bringing into the open things he used to hide.

In the midst of all this attention, Dylan embarked on one of his most famous tours as he headed to London in the summer of 1964. Dylan met the Beatles and hit it off with them, especially John Lennon. (Much later in life, he became very friendly with George Harrison and played with him as part of the Traveling Wilburys.) Since Lennon had already written a book by this point, Dylan sought advice from him in concluding his own book, *Tarantula*.

Dylan was very impressed by British rock, and it is evident in a later London tour, filmed as *Don't Look Back*, that he was particularly taken by the Animals, with their rough blues-rock sound. Dylan must have been particularly impressed with their rendition of "House of the Rising Sun," which was a huge hit in America in August 1964.

That same month, Dylan released his fourth album in two and a half years, *Another Side of Bob Dylan*. The title informed fans of the change Dylan was going through. While the song "The Chimes of Freedom," later covered by the Byrds, would not have been out of place thematically on his previous two albums, the rest of the songs showed a marked shift away from simple folk. Lyrically, the album's centerpiece songs, "All I Really Want to Do," "My Back Pages" (both covered by the Byrds), and "It Ain't Me Babe" (a big hit for the Turtles), are all concerned with love or other personal issues with which Dylan was wrestling. Rather than reflecting and commenting on society, these songs were inspired from within, focusing on Dylan's deepest emotions about love,

Opposite: *Striking a Guthrie pose, Dylan was the new Woody.*

life, his place in the world, and where his future might lie. There is also an anger in "It Ain't Me Babe" that had never before been expressed quite so pointedly in a Dylan song.

Dylan wrote songs that were personal, honest, complex, and mature. Since February 1964, when the Beatles made their American television debut on *The Ed Sullivan Show*, dancing, surfing, cruising, falling in and out of puppy love, and anything else describing what teens spent most of their time doing had been the subjects of most pop songs coming from the Beatles, the British Invasion groups in general, some Motown groups, and the Beach Boys. Writers like Bacharach and David, Goffin and King, Brian Wilson, and occasionally a few others attempted to bring a sophistication to song lyrics and to stretch the musical boundaries, but none came anywhere near Dylan. The aforementioned

Bacharach as well as Buddy Holly, the Everly Brothers, and even Phil Spector were reshaping, expanding, and widening the canvas of arranging and recording popular songs, but none seemed to truly reflect the concerns of the counterculture generation. The inward reflection of the songs Dylan scribed was very new. While the Beatles wrote their own songs and brought a new style and energy to pop music, Dylan's songs had the weight of folk, the imagery of poetry, and the emotional intensity of the blues. This was a whole new approach to song that many of Dylan's folk fans could not understand, especially in songs on *Another Side* that contained any electric instrumentation, which was considered absolute heresy by folk purists. Dylan had changed as an artist forever with this new album; with his next album he would forever change popular music.

Above: *The queen of folk, Joan Baez, and Dylan.* **Opposite:** *Dylan poses for the cover of his 1964 release,* Another Side of Bob Dylan.

CHAPTER THREE

No Direction Home

Opposite: *A rare encounter with a bass guitar, recording* Highway 61 Revisited *in 1965.*
Above: *Contemplating electric guitars in late 1964.*

From the opening whiny, bluesy guitar strains, trash-can drum rhythm, and Dylan's intoning "Johnny's in the basement/Mixing up the medicine/I'm on the pavement/Thinking about the government" in *Bringing It All Back Home*'s "Subterranean Homesick Blues," it was clear to everyone that the times indeed had changed. The song ripped the flimsy veneer of hypocrisy and artifice off the face of postatomic American society. It is both a cautionary warning ("Don't follow leaders/Watch the parkin' meters") and a laundry list of predestined traps and pitfalls ("Twenty years of schoolin'/And they put you on the day shift") that were written with guile, wisdom, and humor. The music is a rollicking, noise-filled blues-rock that was also in many respects the final insult to the old guard folkies.

There are other bluesy rockers on side one, such as "Bob Dylan's 115th Dream," the natural follow-up to "Subterranean Homesick Blues," and "Maggie's Farm," which has a false start that ends in a cacophony of uncontrolled laughter. "Maggie's Farm" is raucous and biting, and may be the all-time take-this-job-and-shove-it anthem. The song, supposedly a true story, could be construed as a farewell to the old folk cabal, a turning away from Dylan's past, or maybe the realization that he had finally made it, professionally and personally, and would never return to the real or intangible prisons that society or anyone wanted to put him in. "On the Road Again" is one of the unheralded gems on the album. Listening to the song, one can easily envision oneself driving in a car through the swamps of the delta, down a deserted curved road with wide, deep ditches on either side. Dylan's ability to authentically reproduce the grit of black blues should not be overlooked, and this song is a startling example.

Side one also contains the poetically beautiful "She Belongs to Me." Amidst the nasty rock, blues edge, and apocalyptic diatribes, Dylan evokes a beautiful melody in this song and in "Love Minus Zero/No Limit," a high-water mark in the evolution of poetry presented in electric popular music. The music on this album is the music that beat poet Allen Ginsberg foresaw in the 1950s and that had a profound influence on the new songs John Lennon wrote with the Beatles.

The second side of the album blends the earlier simplicity of Dylan's acoustic style with an almost surreal lyrical imagery. "Mr. Tambourine Man" has been interpreted, reinterpreted, and examined perhaps more than anything else Dylan had composed until that point. There are many people who feel that the song is about some kind of revelation brought on by the use of drugs; the tambourine man has been seen as the supplier of the chemical potion.

It's hard to say what underlying meaning the song may have, but any interpretation can be considered valid to one's personal point of view,

Two albums like no others released by then in the pop-rock era truly reshaped the artistic expression of the pop or rock song in 1965: *Bringing It All Back Home* in March and *Highway 61 Revisited* in August. Released only five months apart, they expanded the lyrical boundaries of the pop song, became a catalyst for the new genre of folk-rock, and almost single-handedly redefined the role of the singer-songwriter.

Above: *Dylan at the 1964 Newport Folk Festival.*

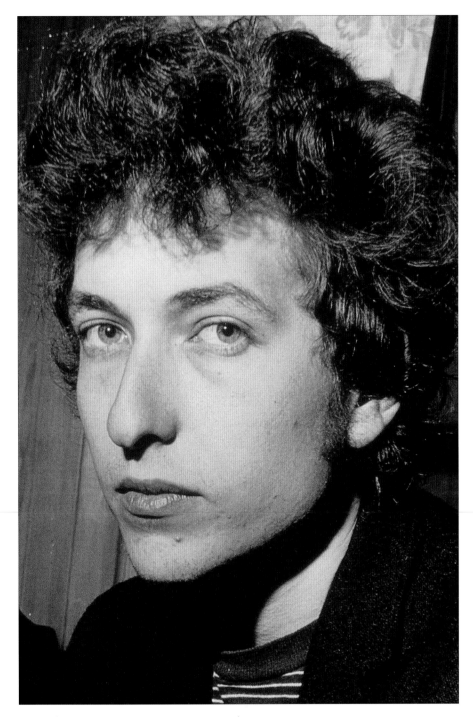

"It's Alright Ma, I'm Only Bleeding" was a bitter song that contained sophisticated rhythmic cadences. The line "But even the president of the United States/Sometimes must have/To stand naked" proved prophetic: when Dylan performed live with the Band on the 1974 *Before the Flood* Tour, the Nixon presidency was unraveling in the wake of Watergate.

The album closed with "It's All Over Now, Baby Blue," another song of a failed relationship, bitterness, and loneliness—and a true classic. The original musical inspiration for the song is surprising. Dylan recalled, "I had carried that song around in my head for a long time and I remember that when I was writing it, I'd remembered a Gene Vincent song. It had always been one of my favorites, 'Baby Blue'....'When first I met my baby, she said how do you do, she looked into my eyes and said...my name is Baby Blue.' It was one of the songs I used to sing back in high school. Of course, I was singing about a different Baby Blue."

Bringing It All Back Home eventually reached number six on the album charts, and Dylan was now a full-fledged member of the rock star aristocracy. He was drawing influences from the likes of the Blues Project (which included Al Kooper, who would play keyboards on his next album), the Butterfield Blues Band (which included Mike Bloomfield, who would play guitar on his next album), and the Byrds.

Perhaps the Byrds would never have been the Byrds if not for Dylan. While the group's look, chiming guitar sound, and harmonies drew more from the Beatles and other groups, Dylan's songs were the core of the group's sensibility. The group had the Dylan connection long before it released its debut album, *Mr. Tambourine Man*, on Columbia Records in June 1965. They met

like the interpretation of any of Dylan's songs. Elaborating on the song for *Biograph*, Dylan said, "Drugs never played a part in that song....'Disappearing in the smoke rings in my mind,' that's not drugs; drugs were never a big thing with me. I could take 'em or leave 'em—never hung me up." Dylan's life at this time was a whirl of recording, performing, writing, traveling, and general craziness, yet out of this chaos he was still able to make the song a thing of monumental strength and beauty.

Above left: *Dylan during the watershed year of 1965 in England.* **Above right:** *The Paul Butterfield Blues Band on the blues workshop stage at the 1965 Newport Folk Festival. From left, Paul Butterfield, Elvin Bishop, Sam Lay, Mike Bloomfield, and Jerome Arnold.*

Dylan in January of that year and were given "Mr. Tambourine Man" to record. The song, which featured studio musicians, Roger McGuinn on guitar, and all the members singing, went to number one and ushered in what became known as folk-rock. The song had the energy and feel of the Beatles, along with folk song narrative intelligence and heady, abstract lyrical textures that were completely new. The Byrds were able to take these disparate styles, bring about the clever Beatles/Dylan synthesis, and completely reshape the musical landscape, foreshadowing the success of Simon and Garfunkel, the Lovin' Spoonful, the Mamas and the Papas, and others. The Byrds' success, coupled with Dylan's already exalted place in music, made Dylan indisputably the single most important American artist in pop music in 1965.

As great as it all seemed, Dylan was still battling many elements in music and in his personal life. Late in 1964, his relationship with Suze long over and his relationship with Joan Baez always rocky, he met Sara Lowndes. Lowndes was a friend of Albert Grossman's wife, Sally, who was living at the Chelsea Hotel with Maria, her daughter from a previous marriage. The relationship with Sara bloomed into a full-fledged love affair.

Dylan embarked on another British tour that was different in many ways. Though Dylan was changing dramatically in the studio, his touring was still

done mostly solo, with an acoustic guitar. This tour was chronicled by D.A. Pennebaker for the film *Don't Look Back*, released in 1967. *Don't Look Back* was a major event in the everchanging myth of Bob Dylan. The film captures Dylan at his most vitriolic when dealing with the press and, in some cases, his fans. In subtle ways it also shows the end of his personal relationship with Joan Baez, and the entrance of Sara into his life. There are plenty of light moments as well, with Dylan dealing with stardom, clowning around, and engaging in sophomoric pranks with sidekick Bob Neuwirth. Not only is the film an important document of one of the most notorious phases in Dylan's evolution, but for all its criticisms, it is important in its depiction of the pop music scene at that time.

Above: *A publicity shot from* Don't Look Back. **Right:** *Dylan spent a lot of time in the studio in 1965.*

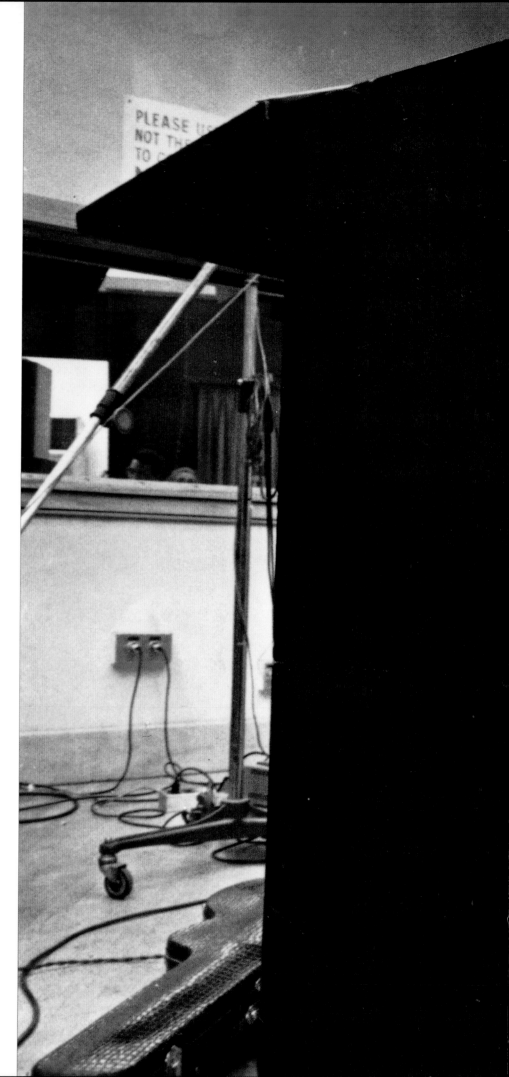

During the summer of 1965, Dylan's rapid change and the shifting perceptions about him continued. One of the key events in Dylan's makeover from folk-protest voice of a generation to poet clown-prince of rock was his appearance at the Newport Folk Festival on July 25. What actually occurred and the circumstances surrounding his appearance there are as clouded in myth and conflicting reports as any moment in Dylan's life.

Having recently become the new darling of the Newport crowd, Dylan appeared at the festival with a huge contingent; when he finally took the stage, the elfin Woody Guthrie hobo had become the epitome of the rock dandy. With the backing of Mike Bloomfield, Jerome Arnold, and Sam Lay—most of the Butterfield Blues Band—as well as Al Kooper and Barry Goldberg, Dylan launched into a raucous new sound for which the staid folk crowd was perhaps not ready. The appearance of Dylan with this lineup apparently was not something that Dylan had planned out well in advance, and not being prepared for how it would sound (technically, not musically) didn't help Dylan win over many of the fans.

While folklore has long had it that Dylan angered the old guard folk organizers of the festival and was booed off the stage, that's not entirely true according to many accounts of that hot July day. Yes, there were boos—but also cheers. Most complained because Dylan and the group were just too loud. And the primitive equipment used was clearly ill-suited for amplified rock, which had the effect of making the words to Dylan's songs almost unintelligible.

Dylan performed "Maggie's Farm" and "Like a Rolling Stone," then left the stage. He returned with just his guitar and proceeded to play "It's All Over Now, Baby Blue" and "Mr. Tambourine Man." How much the less-than-cordial reception of his electric sound figured in his returning with only his guitar may never truly be known. His selection of newer material, though, suggests that Dylan was not about to be dissuaded from bringing his new music to the Newport crowd.

As that turbulent summer wore on Dylan was shifting gears again, and his musical changes would once more have a ripple effect, not only on his music and popularity but in shaping the sound and vision of another group that would leave a mark on rock music: The Band.

The Band—Jamie "Robbie" Robertson, Levon Helm, Rick Danko, Richard Manuel, and Garth Hudson—had been together since 1959. All the members except Helm, were from Canada. They came together as the backing group of Arkansas rockabilly singer Ronnie Hawkins and were initially dubbed the Hawks. Along with backing Hawkins, several members of the group

(continued on page 47)

Left: *At Columbia studios recording* Highway 61 Revisited, *his second album of 1965, with Paul Butterfield Band guitarist Mike Bloomfield.* **Opposite:** *Dylan as the myth was taking shape in the mid-1960s.*

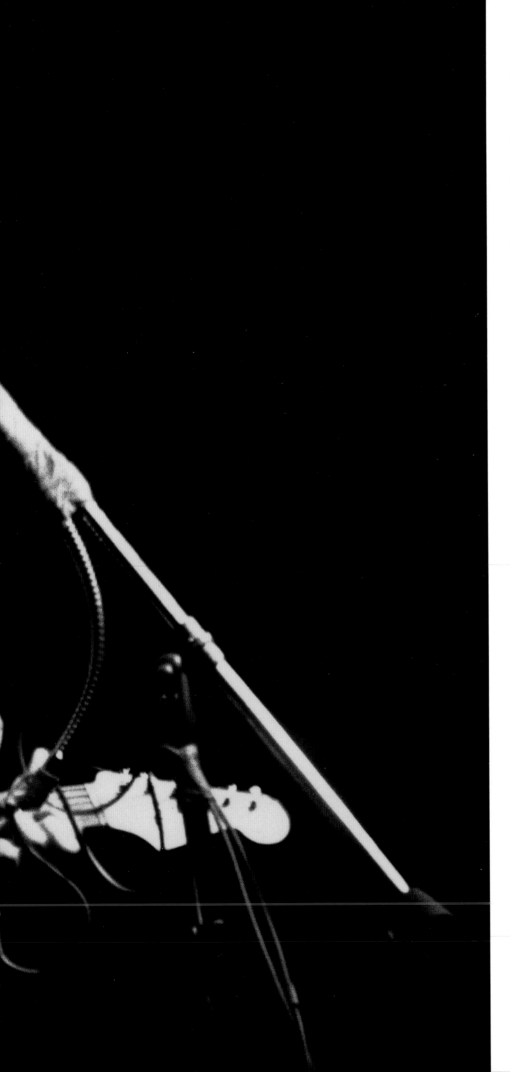

recorded with Mike Bloomfield and John Hammond, Jr., on Hammond's *So Many Roads* album released in 1965. Dylan got together with the group after being introduced to them by Hammond. Some accounts have Dylan hooking up with the group strictly as a result of word of mouth, as he supposedly never actually heard them play before they performed together.

That August Dylan performed at Forest Hills Tennis Stadium in Queens, New York. With Robertson and Helm, along with Al Kooper and Harvey Brooks, Dylan played both acoustic and electric guitar, and this time the audience was more accepting of the change. By the time he reached Carnegie Hall shortly after the Forest Hills show, with "Like a Rolling Stone" all over the radio, his new rock sound was almost unanimously accepted.

Following on the heels of "Like a Rolling Stone," Dylan released *Highway 61 Revisited* in August. On all his music except "Like a Rolling Stone," Dylan was now working with producer Bob Johnston. Except for Dylan's first two albums, Tom Wilson had been Dylan's producer. Johnston seemed to bring a more sure-handed rock feel to the album. On *Bringing It All Back Home*, Dylan still didn't seem entirely comfortable with performing electric rock in the studio. However, it seems that either Johnston's assistance or Dylan's growing confidence with the rock genre made *Highway 61 Revisited* come across as a more relaxed effort.

The album kicks off with "Like a Rolling Stone," with its bullet-shot drum pop, strumming guitar, and Al Kooper's swirling keyboard, which is the song's melodic anchor. The song in many ways signified the musical kickoff of the long journey of the 1960s. It was Dylan's first big hit song and, at around six minutes in length, the longest song ever to hit the Top 40 at that point. The way Dylan described the writing of it, one would never think it would

Pages 44–45: *Albert Grossman, center, Dylan's manager, was never too far from his prize client in 1965.* **Left:** *Dylan and his electric sound were the salvo that declared that rock was where Dylan was and where he was going at Newport, 1965.* **Above:** *An ad for Dylan's notorious single, "Positively 4th Street," in 1965.*

New York. Both this version and the version Judy Collins did many years later on her *In My Life* album illustrate the universal appeal and timelessness of the story and the music. The album closes with the long, sprawling "Desolation Row," another apocalyptic vision perfectly suited to the growing antiwar sentiments and tensions that were fervently spreading across America.

Although the Beatles released their brilliant *Rubber Soul* album (clearly influenced by Dylan with its surreal lyrics and overall folk music sound) in 1965, no other artists on either side of the Atlantic could possibly have had more influence on other musicians and their music than Dylan and his two latest albums. With all the success, adulation, and attention, the pressures of stardom were getting to Dylan, and around this time he composed one of his most biting songs, "Positively 4th Street." Written only days after his Newport appearance, it was a swipe at the old folk crowd. (The song would not appear on an album until the March 1967 release of his first set of greatest hits.)

The year ended on a positive note for Dylan. On November 11 he married Sara, and his next album, *Blonde on Blonde*, released in May 1966, contained many songs of his new love, the inspiration for perhaps his greatest album—easily one of the top five rock albums ever made, according to many music journalists.

become so revolutionary a song: "My wife [Sara Lowndes] and I lived in a little cabin in Woodstock, which we rented from Peter Yarrow's mother. I wrote the song there, in this cabin. We had come up from New York, and I had about three days off up there to get some stuff together [for the next album]. It just came, you know. It started with that 'La Bamba' riff."

"Tombstone Blues" is a rollicking, out-of-control, apocalyptic carnival of sound created by Bloomfield's dazzling guitar work. Dylan said he'd "felt like I'd broken through with this song, that nothing like it had been done before...just a flash really." "It Takes a Lot to Laugh, It Takes a Train to Cry," has an almost western saloon sound with its clanky piano. "From a Buick 6," with its blues-rock sound, is a musical cousin of "Maggie's Farm." "Ballad of a Thin Man," with its sinister piano and guitar and spooky organ swirls, introduced Mr. Jones to the rock vocabulary and was part of the cultural sorting-out of the straights and the freaks.

Side two of the *Highway 61 Revisited* album begins with the lovely, bittersweet, and revealing "Queen Jane Approximately," a song filled with aching desire and complexities beyond anything anyone had written as a love song at that time. The title track is a rambling, raucous song that has the apocalyptic lyrical visions of "Tombstone Blues." For all its obscure references, "Just Like Tom Thumb's Blues" appears highly autobiographical and personal. The song is essentially about Dylan's travels and how he needed to get back home—back to

Above left: *Dylan with Baez during a photo session for the* Highway 61 Revisited *album cover.* **Above right:** *With his rock and roll look, it was clear the Newport Folk Festival in 1965 would be a big change for Dylan.*

Blonde on Blonde was a remarkable achievement: two albums of music that were funny, bitter, sweet, surreal, and ambitious, to say the least. Dylan has often been compared to Picasso for many reasons, and this album shows him painting on a broad canvas: he created with words the way Picasso, who changed, rearranged, and distorted images to create his own vision, created with paint. Perhaps no other album had made people think about their lives, their loves, and the basic meaning of their own existence as much until that time. More than thirty years later, the album resonates just as powerfully as it did upon its release.

For Dylan the album was, more than anything, about his love for Sara. The feelings of tenderness and desire are unmistakable, but there is also regret, loneliness, and a detachment from his subject that demonstrates the pain and frustration in any relationship. Dylan had gone very far to try to express the true complexities of love in the most honest way possible, and it is that honesty that makes this album timeless.

Ironically, for a recording filled with love songs and beautiful melodies, Dylan, in his amusing way, opens the album with "Rainy Day Women #12 & 35," a funny, boozy party song that has probably clocked in more dorm-room party time than any other song, except maybe for "Louie Louie." The "everybody must get stoned" chorus would join "I get high with a little help from my friends" by the Beatles as the two most notorious nods to "mind expansion" in the pop lexicon.

From there, the album is almost exclusively filled with torch songs for the new generation. "Pledging My Time" is a bluesy love song of uncompromising devotion, while "Visions of Johanna" is filled with obscure poetic images that many suggested were the result of a drug experience. "One of Us Must Know" is one of Dylan's most underrated songs. Its unique take on love and relationships melodically prefigures "Idiot Wind," and shows Dylan both stretching out musically and writing concise folk-rock-flavored pop.

"I Want You," the last song recorded for the *Blonde on Blonde* sessions, is another song of concise pop, filled with honest desire and Dylan's wonderful harmonica work. "Stuck Inside of Mobile with the Memphis Blues Again" is masterfully arranged, with unforgettable choruses. The long, sprawling track, which has wonderful guitar interplay, alludes to Dylan and Grossman's ever-deteriorating relationship with the lines "An' he just smoked my eyelids/An' punched my cigarette," no doubt referring to the odd way Grossman smoked a cigarette. "Leopard Skin Pill-Box Hat," which Dylan is still performing with gusto today, is a big rockin' blues number in the Chicago style. "Just Like a Woman" (like later songs such as "Forever Young," "Lay Lady Lay," and "Knockin' on Heaven's Door") was a song of such universality that to simply

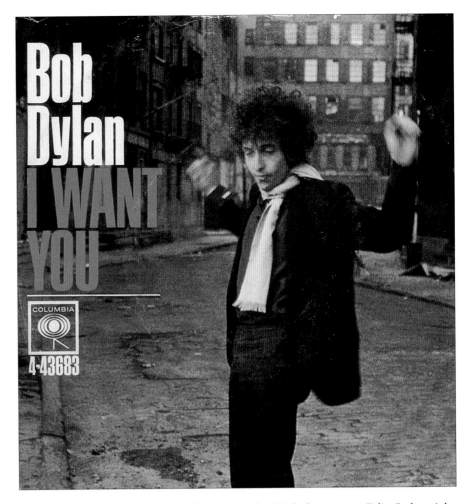

say it was inspired by the pained life of Andy Warhol scenester Edie Sedgewick gives it short shrift.

On the second album Dylan continues the raucous blues-rock feel with "Most Likely You Go Your Way and I'll Go Mine," and expands on the Butterfield Blues influence in "Obviously 5 Believers." A softer side comes through in the slow piano blues of "Temporary Like Achilles" and in the lilting waltz of "4th Time Around." "Absolutely Sweet Marie," replete with loneliness and pining, is another song still performed with passion by Dylan.

The album closes with the twelve-minute, side-length "Sad-Eyed Lady of the Lowlands," an epic love elegy to Sara that is heartbreaking in its beauty and astounding in its breadth and ambition—and that unfortunately, because of its length and somewhat obscure nature, has been one of Dylan's most misunderstood songs.

With the release of these three albums in less than eighteen months, Dylan had completely moved away from folk, forever changed the lyrical language of rock, and become the single most important American figure in rock music. In only a short time, though, it all changed.

Above: *A rare picture sleeve for the single, "I Want You."*

CHAPTER FOUR

Woodstock Skyline

Opposite: *Dylan in the 1966 D.A. Pennebaker film,* Eat the Document.
Above: *Dylan attempting to shield himself from the pressure-cooker of 1966 at the Hotel George V in Paris.*

anyone to take. Photographs of Dylan at the time compared to those taken many months later showed a dramatic difference. Dylan was thin, gaunt, troubled-looking, and almost crazed in his countenance. Later photos reveal a healthier, fleshier man, seemingly at peace—the man and now-father that he was, rather than the elfin court jester of rock.

On July 30, 1966, while Dylan drove his Triumph 500 motorcycle along a road near his house, he lost control and had a bad spill. Various reports had him suffering everything from amnesia to a broken neck as well as a concussion, lacerations, a period of unconsciousness, and temporary partial paralysis. Thankfully, his condition turned out to be not so serious, and after a week in the hospital and a month of bed rest at home, he was fine.

The timing of the accident, in an odd twist of fate, may have been fortuitous. Dylan's lifestyle, schedule, and various sources of pressure were pushing his emotional and physical endurance limits and maybe only something so cataclysmic could have slowed him down. Others in Dylan's circle had lost their lives. Richard Farina, a gifted singer-songwriter, a journalist, and the author of the eerily prophetic novel *Been Down So Long, It Looks Like Up to Me,* who had been married to Joan Baez's sister Mimi, had died in a motorcycle accident. Paul Clayton, a close friend and someone Dylan had shared many stages with, had jumped out a window after a three-day acid trip. And the talented folk artist Pete LaFarge, one of the most beloved figures of the Village folk scene, had committed suicide. The precarious business of being an artist had taken and would continue to take many young men and women much too soon in those crystalline days. Fortunately for Bob Dylan and all his fans, he was not one of them.

After the accident, Dylan spent most of his time with his wife and kids, catching up on reading and just enjoying the escape from the star-maker machinery in which Grossman had him so wrapped up. As 1966 drew to a close, Dylan and the pop scene went in two very different directions. While the new culture of the 1960s caught the fancy of the press and the masses it had been building toward for years, the music Dylan was making was very different from the other pop and underground music of the day and was not officially released for eight years. It had a profound influence, nonetheless.

In March 1967, Columbia issued *Bob Dylan's Greatest Hits* to compensate for Dylan's absence on the music scene. Complete with the now famous Milton Glaser rainbow poster, the album further fueled the prevalent speculation that maybe Dylan would never record or perform again. The myth makers, storytellers, and gossip columnists in and out of the counterculture speculated endlessly about what happened to Dylan after his accident. All kinds of bizarre reports from the ridiculous to the sick circulated.

After *Blonde on Blonde*, Dylan retreated to Byrdcliffe, his house in Woodstock, where he attempted to find some peace from the hectic demands of pop stardom. In this idyllic setting, though, a near tragedy struck that is part and parcel of the Dylan myth in that what actually happened, how it was perceived, and what effect it had on Dylan personally are shrouded in conjecture.

Clearly Dylan's health was not at its best. How or why this was the case is pure speculation. The frantic touring and the demands of writing, recording, and whatever else Grossman lined up for him may have been too much for

Above: *Dylan performing in the late 1960s.*

That summer, the group formerly known as the Hawks and now officially dubbed The Band moved their families to a rented house in West Saugerties, New York, not too far from Dylan's house. Named after the color it was painted, the house was called Big Pink. This bland, more suburban than country, small split-level became one of the most important physical landmarks in all of rock music history. Due to some of the music that was written, talked about, performed, and later remembered there, it became the Graceland of the North and, for all intent and purposes, the house that gave birth to The Band.

To understand how revolutionary the next phase of Dylan's career was, it is important to understand what was going on in the hazy summer of 1967. San Francisco had become the epicenter of the 1960s cultural revolution. The Haight-Ashbury district was seen as the Eden of the hippie movement, with Bill Graham's Fillmore and other ballrooms such as the Avalon serving as the gardens of musical delights. The San Francisco sound, spearheaded by the Jefferson Airplane, the Grateful Dead, Quicksilver Messenger Service, the

(continued on page 57)

Above: *One more cup of coffee: Dylan in May of 1966 at the Hotel George V in Paris.*

Charlatans, and Big Brother and the Holding Company, among many others, was defining the new acid rock. Down the coast the Monterey Pop Festival—the first time many would see and hear Janis Joplin, Jimi Hendrix, and the Who—occurred from June 16 to 18 at almost the same moment the Beatles released the mother of all concept albums, *Sgt. Pepper's Lonely Hearts Club Band*. Style, drugs, electronics, volume, and of course peace and love swept through the counterculture and beyond that summer, as Scott McKenzie recommended to anyone heading to San Francisco and all points hip to wear flowers in their hair. While the age of Aquarius was dawning in all its incense-burning, caftan-flowing, sandal-wearing, long-haired heaviness, Dylan and the five members of The Band were making music that was never intended to be heard by the public.

The members of The Band had played with Dylan on and off over the previous year or so in different configurations. Robertson, Danko, Manuel, and Hudson had played a great deal, but Helm, reportedly not all that thrilled with the less-than-enthusiastic response many of the shows received, especially in England, was sometimes replaced by Mickey Jones, a drummer who had played with Trini Lopez.

Big Pink was not the original recording location for what came to be known as *The Basement Tapes*. The initial recordings took place a few miles away at Dylan's house in what was oddly called the red room. Recording at Big Pink finally got under way with microphones borrowed from Peter, Paul and Mary, and a tape recorder and two stereo mixing consoles on loan from Grossman. The recordings were made for several reasons, mostly just to have fun and give Dylan and The Band a chance to make music away from the confines and pressures of the recording studio and the concert stage. Dylan did not tour, as it turned out, for another eight years, other than the occasional performance. These recordings were demos of new songs that Dylan had written or was writing, with fourteen of the reported one hundred eventually pressed onto acetate to be heard by other musicians who might want to record them, including the Manfred Mann hit "Quinn the Eskimo"; "You Ain't Goin' Nowhere," the lead-off track of the Byrds' 1968 release, *Sweetheart of the Rodeo* (the one and only Byrds album that featured Gram Parsons, and for many the first country-rock album); and "Too Much of Nothing," recorded by Peter, Paul and Mary. The often bootlegged recording called *The Basement Tapes*, in its unedited entirety, included much more music than the official 1975 double-album release, which was made up of sixteen *Basement* recordings and eight Band demos. These recordings and Dylan's later infamous *Great White Wonder* were in many respects the beginning of the bootleg recording underground.

The music itself was very different from both the exploding, psychedelic acid-rock of the day and the music Dylan had made on his three previous studio albums. In fact, it had more in common with Dylan's earliest influences of country, folk, blues, and other sounds from the earlier part of the century—and even from the nineteenth century. If the pop music of the day was multi-colored Day-Glo, *The Basement Tapes* was black and white and gray, burnished in brown and honey sepia tones. There was a richness and a warmth to it, with an edge of grit, honesty, and folk amateurishness. It was odd, yet familiar—old, but timeless. The music also had more in common with the sound The Band made on its early albums. After listening to *The Basement Tapes*, The Band's first few albums, and the post–*Blonde on Blonde* Dylan albums, it's hard to tell who actually influenced whom.

Along with the old songs played for fun, there were songs recorded that would make up an important part of future projects. Dylan's composition "I Shall Be Released" turned up on The Band's debut, *Music from Big Pink*, and would, along with the traditional "We Shall Overcome" and Dylan's own later composition "Forever Young," become a timeless anthem of hope, celebration, and bravery. "Forever Young," one of Dylan's most touching compositions, according to the *Biograph* notes, came rather quickly and unexpectedly: "I wrote [the song] in Tucson. I wrote it thinking about one of my boys and not wanting to be too sentimental. The lines came to me; they were done in a minute. I don't know. Sometimes that's what you're given. You're given something like that. You don't know what it is exactly that you want but this is what comes. That's how that song came out. I certainly didn't intend to write it—I was going for something else. The song wrote itself—naw, you never know what you're going to write. You never even know if you're going to make another record, really."

There are two songs that Dylan cowrote with members of The Band that also made it to The Band's debut album. "Tears of Rage" is a mournful ballad that conjures up a long-lost America from, perhaps, the 1800s. "This Wheel's on Fire" is jauntier but no less reflective in its sense of looking back to another time—another song of timeless eloquence. In the liner notes of *The Basement Tapes*, Dylan described the music from the sessions and his kinship with the blues: "With a certain kind of blues music, you can sit down and play it....you may have to lean forward a little."

The easygoing playing and attitude that went into these recordings are obvious, but this is not to suggest that they are frivolous. These were recordings started by a man who had been at the top of the new rock game, who had faced death, and who was seeking the companionship of like-minded musicians, who themselves were piecing together what would become their own

Pages 54–55: *Dylan at a press conference at the Hotel George V in Paris.* **Opposite:** *In 1966, at the zenith of his pop stardom, Dylan contemplates Hamlet's Castle Krönborg in May 1966, as he is about to launch his world tour.*

unique, everlasting collective sound. These recordings are a real key to the Dylan story. Dylan arrived at this place after years of immersing himself in the music of country, blues, folk, rock, and pop. It is his love of the songs, singers, and players that still sustains him, right up to today. He is the true working musician, and the sessions for *The Basement Tapes* marked perhaps the first time he fully realized it. There was also no other group of musicians like The Band, who connected with Dylan in the same way, musically and spiritually.

On the heels of the sessions of *The Basement Tapes*, Dylan returned to Nashville to record his next album. While many saw this as a major change for

Dylan, it was not: *Blonde on Blonde* had been recorded in Nashville, and country elements in Dylan's music were nothing new. Recorded in October 1967 and released in December of that year, *John Wesley Harding* was almost grim compared to the orgy of pop, rock, and blues on *Blonde on Blonde*. Dylan's decision to borrow the name of the western outlaw John Wesley Harding is one clear indication of how profound an impact *The Basement Tapes* had on him. During those sessions the group had recorded many songs from the early part of the century whose stories were rooted in even earlier times. The image of the fading West—or more accurately of old ways, before technology, the

Opposite: *Dylan and his wife, Sara, at the Isle of Wight concert.* **Above:** *Only weeks after Woodstock, Dylan came out of his self-imposed performing exile at the Isle of Wight festival in England, September 1969.*

bomb, and rampant, unchecked, media-fueled consumerism took hold—may have been what Dylan was musing on. The outlaw image, even the exile, was a perfect metaphor for Dylan himself. Maybe he just liked the sound of the music. The photo on the album cover shows Dylan surrounded by what look like Indians or mountain men, and he's smiling! Insight into Dylan's state of mind at the time is hard to figure, and the man himself wasn't offering many clues.

The music on the album was a mixed bag, with backing from bassist Charles McCoy and drummer Kenny Buttrey along with Pete Drake on steel guitar on the romantic "I'll Be Your Baby Tonight" and "Down Along the Cove." "All Along the Watchtower" could have come from any of Dylan's earlier albums and, as interpreted by Jimi Hendrix, went on to become one of the staples of the new psychedelic pop landscape. Hendrix had done other Dylan songs, such as "Drifters Escape," "Like a Rolling Stone," and "Crawl Out Your Window." Dylan has admitted that he now performs "All Along the Watchtower" the way Hendrix did it as somewhat of a tribute to the late legend. Also on the album were "Dear Landlord," "I Am a Lonesome Hobo," and "I Pity the Poor Immigrant," more songs that would not have been out of place on any of his earlier albums and that were inspired by the dust bowl ballads of his hero, Woody Guthrie. There were songs that were clearly inspired by the Bible and other religious writings, such as the aforementioned "All Along the Watchtower" as well as "I Dreamed I Saw St. Augustine" and "The Ballad of Frankie Lee and Judas Priest."

For many, *John Wesley Harding* was a disappointment, although the album did receive many good reviews. From that point on, many compared Dylan's post–motorcycle accident recordings to the recordings Elvis Presley made after he left the army. The music didn't live up to Dylan's previous recordings and some of the spark was gone. Also, in relation to the flash and din of psychedelia and the mounting power of the counterculture, the music didn't address the broader national and world issues of the day. Such criticism was unfortunately shortsighted, and again, maybe Dylan was just moving too fast for his audience; in hindsight, *John Wesley Harding* is a worthy addition to the Dylan canon.

Upon the release of the album, Dylan made a rare concert appearance with The Band at a Carnegie Hall concert for Woody Guthrie. Around that time the mortality that Dylan had been grappling with since his motorcycle accident really hit home when his father died. What kind of relationship he had had with his father is unknown, but certainly his father's death was a devastating blow that probably pushed him further inside himself.

Right: *Dylan with other Isle of Wight performers, Rick Danko (left) and Robbie Robertson (right) of The Band. This was Dylan's first live performance after his motorcycle accident.*

The warm glow of 1967 had long faded, only to be replaced by the white heat of violence that gripped the United States in 1968, and Dylan remained ensconced in his own domestic happiness in Woodstock. The assassinations of the Reverend Martin Luther King, Jr., and Bobby Kennedy; the riots at the Democratic National Convention; and the escalation of the war in Vietnam and the growing certainty that Richard Nixon would become president of the United States drew no musical response from Dylan. As author David Caute so perfectly described it in the title of his book on 1968, it was "the year of the barricades." It is hard to figure out why Dylan, who had so perfectly encapsulated the sixties in his songs, had nothing to say musically about the decade, now that the tears of rage had erupted into murder, violence, and brutality. Perhaps Dylan did not have to say anything more. Hadn't his songs foretold of this apocalyptic moment? Hadn't he already stated that we were right in the middle of becoming the new generation and anyone not busy being born would be dying? Still, one wonders if somehow he was afraid himself of the violence then so rampant, afraid for his own safety and that of his family, and wanted no part of the unfolding explosion of insanity.

Nixon won the presidency in November 1968 with the promise to end the war in Vietnam—which proved to be false—as well as to restore law and order, a code that middle-class voters understood as a call to crack down on hippie agitators and antiwar demonstrators. Dylan returned to Nashville and this time made an even more overtly country album. Released in April 1969, *Nashville Skyline* was another album that disheartened those who looked to Dylan as the voice of a generation. Captured beautifully in a photograph by Elliot Landy, Dylan is smiling on the album cover with guitar in hand, touching his hat in a gesture of greeting, perhaps to suggest, "Come and sit with me and I'll play you some songs." The music on the album reflects just such a mood. The opening track, "Girl from the North Country," written for his high school sweetheart, Echo, was originally recorded on his second album. On *Nashville Skyline*, the song is sung with Johnny Cash, and Dylan's voice is warm and honeyed rather than biting and croaky. "Lay Lady Lay" is another beautiful love song, obviously written for Sara. The song that perhaps best encapsulates this whole period for Dylan is the closing track, "Tonight I'll Be Staying Here with You," perhaps expressing Dylan's reluctance to be part of or comment on the hurly-burly cultural, social, and political upheavals of the day and his desire to just be safe and secure in the love of his wife and children.

After a period of relative obscurity, Dylan began to become a bit more active and available in 1969. He performed on Johnny Cash's television special, but did not appear at the Woodstock festival. Oddly enough, the producers of the event initially envisioned building a recording studio in the Woodstock

Above: *Dylan at a press conference at New York's Kennedy Airport in September 1969 for the Isle of Wight festival.*

area because musicians like Dylan lived there; instead, however, they ended up producing the festival. The Band did perform, but their manager, Albert Grossman, would not allow their performance to be included in the film or on the album in order to keep the group's mystique intact.

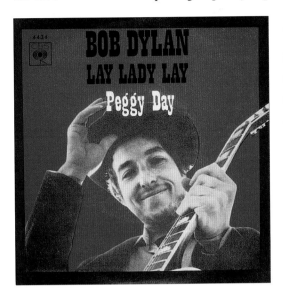

Dylan moved back to the Village that summer, perhaps in an effort to rekindle the spirit of his old folk days. He appeared at the Isle of Wight Music festival in September; he came on very late and was not met with a warm reception. He gave an interview to *Rolling Stone* magazine around this time in which he described himself as "just a musician," a stance he maintained for years to come.

The following summer, Dylan received an honorary doctorate from Princeton University. In June, he released a double album, *Self Portrait*, which was all cover songs and which largely disappointed his fans. He returned in October with *New Morning*, his most well received album since his motorcycle accident. The songs it contained were more in line with what could be expected from Dylan in quality and subject. "If Not for You" was another great love song, and it was covered perfectly by George Harrison on his first solo recording, *All Things Must Pass*, also released in 1970. The title cut brought back some of the bite to Dylan's voice and signaled a renewed energy. For all the renewed energy, it also marked a change: Dylan eventually moved on to new management. He had a falling out with Grossman in June 1971 over control of his songs, which led him to look for a new manager and a new record label. Dylan did not release another album of all-new material until he reunited with The Band for his new record deal with Asylum Records in 1974 and came out with *Planet Waves*.

The 1970s saw Dylan go through many changes, and much like in the 1960s, they woud both counterbalance and mirror the changes American society was going through. And in the middle of the decade, he made what many consider to be perhaps his best album: *Blood on the Tracks*.

Above left: *A rare cover for Dylan's big single, "Lay Lady Lay."* **Above right:** *A painting by Dylan for* Sing Out! *magazine 1968.*

CHAPTER FIVE

Bringing It All Back Home

Opposite: *Dylan during the* Before the Flood *tour in 1974.* **Above:** *Having fun with Arlo (left), the son of his hero Woody Guthrie, and another early mentor, Dave Van Ronk (right).*

change through music that was a major part of the 1960s cultural explosion. It makes sense that such an event simply had to include Bob Dylan. If there was a musical figure of the sixties who best represented bringing about hope and change for the downtrodden, it was Dylan. His surprise performance was nothing short of transcendent, and for many his appearance at the event rekindled his stature as a committed artist, and was a sign that he was clearly back with all his musical power and social consciousness intact.

Pete Fornatale, an author and teacher who is best known as one of the rock deejays of WNEW-FM in New York since 1969 (with a short stint at WXRK-FM), recalled Dylan's surprise performance in his 1987 book, *The Story of Rock 'n' Roll:* "It was a truly star-studded event before a spellbound audience. Everyone's senses were totally immersed in the enjoyment of rock legends George Harrison, Ringo Starr, Eric Clapton, Leon Russell, Billy Preston, and others. There had been rumors beforehand of other possible guests at the concert, but most of them centered around the possibility of a never-to-be Beatles reunion. So I, for one, was taken totally by surprise that afternoon when I noticed out of the corner of my eye a familiar, curly-haired, denim-clad figure with an acoustic guitar and harmonica making his way to center stage to begin an unannounced, unexpected performance. It was Dylan, of course, with a mesmerizing five-song set that dazzled the assembled multitude."

The 1970s began with a burst of recording activity for Dylan, with the disappointing *Self Portrait* in June and a return to form on *New Morning* that October. In August 1971, Dylan made a surprise concert appearance that firmly reestablished his magnetism as a performer.

George Harrison prepared a concert to raise funds for the starving multitudes of flood-ravaged Bangladesh through his friendship with Indian sitar master Ravi Shankar. The event included such rock royalty as Ringo Starr and Eric Clapton, among many others. Future album and film projects also raised funds for Bangladesh, and the concert was the forerunner of such later megagatherings of the 1980s as Live Aid, Farm Aid, and Freedom Fest, to name a few. These events grew out of a sense of bringing about political and social

Above left: *Dylan makes a surprise appearance at the Concert for Bangledesh in August 1971.* **Above right:** *Dylan received an honorary degree from Princeton University in 1970.*

Shortly thereafter, in November, Columbia released *Bob Dylan's Greatest Hits, Volume II*. The double album contained just about every popular cut of Dylan's up to that point that was not on the first volume and, like that first album, included some material not on previous albums. There were two tracks produced by Leon Russell: "When I Paint My Masterpiece," covered by the Band on *Cahoots* with some new lyrics, and "Watching the River Flow," which perfectly captured the new fire in Dylan's songwriting. There were also two other songs from *The Basement Tapes* sessions, as well as "I Shall Be Released,"

which Dylan had recorded in October and on which Woodstock inhabitant Happy Traum supplied help on bass, banjo, guitar, and harmony. Also featured was a 1963 recording from Carnegie Hall of "Tomorrow Is a Long Time."

Dylan began playing on lots of sessions and also occasionally dropped in on live performances in the Village and elsewhere, supplying musical support on a wide variety of instruments for many artists. In January 1972, the *Concert for Bangladesh* multialbum box set was released, and Dylan's performances of "A Hard Rain's A-Gonna Fall," "Blowin' in the Wind," "Mr. Tambourine

Above: *Performing with George Harrison at the Bangladesh concert.*

Man," and "It Takes a Lot to Laugh, It Takes a Train to Cry" were easily the highlights of both the album and the film made about the concert.

Although Dylan had been filmed before and could easily be called the star of *Don't Look Back*, late 1972 began his first foray into dramatic feature film acting. Sam Peckinpah, the king of intellectual action movies, was about to film *Pat Garrett & Billy the Kid* in Durango, Mexico, starring James Coburn and Kris Kristofferson. At the urging of Kristofferson, and after having seen and liked some of Peckinpah's films, Dylan joined the cast and was also slated to supply music for the film. The story was about William Bonney, also known as Billy the Kid, and Pat Garrett. Dylan played a cameo role as a printer's assistant named Alias, who was Billy the Kid's helper. Dylan commented on the

film in the *Biograph* notes: "Actually, I was just one of Peckinpah's pawns. There wasn't a part for me and Sam just liked me around....Rudy Wurlitzer, who was writing this thing, invented a part for me but there wasn't any dimension to it and I was very uncomfortable in this non-role....The music seemed to be scattered and used in every other place but the scenes in which we did it for. Except for 'Knockin' on Heaven's Door,' I can't say as though I recognized anything I'd done being in the place that I'd done it for."

Dylan moved his family down to Durango and recorded all of the music for the film there in January 1973. The original soundtrack recording was released in July 1973 and yielded the huge hit "Knockin' on Heaven's Door." The song would have fit in nicely on *Nashville Skyline* as it had a big cinematic sound, and it proved again that Dylan had a rich, full voice. For the most part, the music (mostly instrumental), Dylan's performance, and the film received positive reviews; despite this, it was a long time before Dylan acted in another film. However, it soon became apparent that making films interested Dylan.

With Dylan's Columbia contract expired in 1973 and Clive Davis unceremoniously ousted as head of Columbia Records, the label issued an album called *Dylan* in time for that Christmas. Including leftovers from the *Self Portrait* and *New Morning* sessions, but no Dylan compositions, the album was easily the worst ever issued with Dylan's name on it. Exactly who was responsible for allowing it to be released to an unsuspecting public is still not clear.

Overshadowing the November release of *Dylan* was word that Dylan was about to embark on his first tour in more than eight years with backing from The Band. The tour, which came to be known as Tour '74, began in January in Chicago and proved to be quite different from the previous tours Dylan and The Band had done. By then, The Band had become one of the most critically acclaimed groups around, due to such albums as *Music from Big Pink*, *The Band*, and the live double album *Rock of Ages*, and the tour was being produced by San Francisco rock impresario Bill Graham of Fillmore fame. It proved to be a monumental success. The group flew from city to city aboard a forty-seat chartered 707 christened *Starship 1*. The tour covered twenty-one cities and played thirty-nine shows over a six-week period. The shows consisted of a combination of Dylan playing with The Band, The Band playing alone, and an acoustic set with Dylan performing solo with just a guitar. Coming not long after The Band played with the Allman Brothers Band and the Grateful Dead at the Watkins Glen festival, the tour, along with a cross-country trek by Crosby, Stills, Nash and Young, signified the birth of what would become de rigueur for superstar acts: playing mammoth tours in arenas and stadiums, with massive technical and personnel support. These concerts were events the size and scope of which had previously only been matched at the likes of Newport,

Above: *In Sam Peckinpah's film,* Pat Garrett & Billy the Kid *(1972), Dylan had his chance to be in a western, something he dreamed about as a boy.* **Opposite:** *Dylan in a scene from* Pat Garrett & Billy the Kid.

Monterey, Woodstock, the Isle of Wight, Bangladesh, and Watkins Glen. As successful as the shows appeared to be, Dylan was less than enthusiastic about the tour when remembering it in the *Biograph* booklet: "We were hoping to do an extremely different kind of show. But we rehearsed and eventually settled on a show that wasn't dissimilar from our last tours [in 1965 and 1966]. But this time when we played, everybody loved us. I don't know if we needed it but it was kind of a relief."

Dylan continued, "I think I was just playing a role on that tour. I was playing Bob Dylan and The Band was playing The Band. It was sort of mindless. The people that came out to see us came mostly to see what they missed the first time around. It was just more of a 'legendary' kind of thing. They've heard about it, they'd bought the records, whatever, but what they saw didn't give any clue to what was."

The tour and Dylan's ongoing relationship with The Band yielded the only two albums he recorded for a label other than Columbia, both released in 1974 on David Geffen's Asylum label. There was *Before the Flood*, released in June, a live double album of performances from shows recorded in New York, Seattle, Oakland, and Los Angeles that was a fine representation of the shows' success. *Planet Waves*, out since January, continued Dylan's rejuvenation and included the jaunty "On a Night Like This." Also on this album is "Forever Young," the quintessential ode from a father to his child, written for his son Jesse, which is included on the album in two different tempos.

Dylan's continuing emergence came about at a time when songwriters had come to dominate the rock landscape. Since the dawn of the 1970s, aside from a handful of bands, singer-songwriters were the artists who were gaining the most commercial and critical notice and who were also capturing the bulk of FM airplay. The most dominant tastemakers of the day were magazines like *Rolling Stone* and what had been underground FM radio in the sixties—which was mutating into album rock radio. The center of hip musical activity was the West Coast, although clearly the scenes in London and New York were still important musical meccas. After the barrage of the sixties, music was becoming quieter and more introspective. The Nixon presidency, the Vietnam War, and the other big issues of the day were beginning to or had already come to a conclusion, and the sixties generation was looking back at its own past, where it was heading, and how the public and personal events of the past would shape its ultimate destiny. Artists like Cat Stevens, James Taylor, Elton John, Jackson Browne, Joni Mitchell, Neil Young, and countless others were pouring their hearts out in simple confessionals that brought a maturity and a personal vision to music that was a far cry from the flag-waving yell of sixties revolutionary rock. Certainly Dylan had a tremendous impact on all of these artists with the

Left: *Rick Danko, Robbie Robertson, Levon Helm, and Dylan on the 1974 Dylan and The Band tour, documented on the* Before the Flood *album.*

way he expanded the language of the pop song and brought an honesty to the lyrics that erased the mere escapism of much of pop music.

At this point in the decade, with enormous civil rights gains achieved, Nixon out of the White House, and American involvement in the Vietnam War almost at an end, Dylan released *Blood on the Tracks* in January 1975. As great as *Bringing It All Back Home, Highway 61 Revisited,* and *Blonde on Blonde* were, *Blood on the Tracks* was a 1970s rock masterpiece.

Dylan had begun recording the album in September 1974 in New York, with Buddy Cage, Tony Brown, Paul Griffin, and Eric Weissberg and his band Deliverance, but eventually re-recorded all but three songs in Minneapolis with

additional support from musicians Bill Peterson, Ken Odegard, Bill Berg, Greg Imhofer, and Chris Weber. The notes that accompanied the album package made it very unclear which musicians actually played on which tracks, and some issues do not include Pete Hamill's brilliant liner notes, which eventually won a Grammy.

Dylan returned to Columbia in 1975 as his Asylum albums were selling poorly and he was getting pressure from David Geffen to develop a better-selling album. *Blood on the Tracks,* Dylan's first official release back with Columbia, is many things. Most observers, Dylan watchers, and critics agree that the album is a chronicle of Dylan's disintegrating marriage to Sara.

Above: *The SNACK (Students Need Athletics, Culture, and Kids) Concert in 1975.* **Opposite:** *Dylan in concert at Nassau Coliseum, 1974.*

However, in the annotated *Biograph* notes, particularly in response to the song "You're a Big Girl Now," Dylan stated, " 'You're a Big Girl Now,' well, I read that this was supposed to be about my wife. I wish somebody would ask me first before they go ahead and print stuff like that. I mean it couldn't be about anybody else but my wife, right?...I'm a mystery only to those who haven't felt the same things I have." As bitter as such songs as "You're a Big Girl Now" and "Idiot Wind" are, much of the music, such as "Simple Twist of Fate," "You're Gonna Make Me Lonesome When You Go," and "If You See Her, Say Hello," revealed Dylan's pain at the inevitable end of this great love due to his rock star lifestyle and almost constant touring.

Dylan has never admitted whether the album was about Sara or not, but his divorce in June 1977 would have to indicate such was the case. Lyrically, the album was a look back at the 1960s. "Tangled Up in Blue" is clearly a meditation on where the journey of the sixties had led many people, as well as a remembrance of those days. The lyrics of all the songs are rich in poetic imagery and, except for "You're Gonna Make Me Lonesome When You Go," don't contain any of the surreal imagery of Dylan's mid-sixties music. These are songs rich in story, with a clear narrative, sung with a conviction that years after the album's release is still as poignant as ever.

Musically, *Blood on the Tracks* is one of Dylan's most consistent efforts. Engineered by Phil Ramone, who has worked with such other big names as Billy Joel and Paul Simon, the album is slick and crisp, with clean acoustic guitar work and emotional phrasing from Dylan that once and for all proves him to be not a good singer, but a great singer. For an artist who often reveals nothing of his personal life to the press—or to anyone for that matter—the album is highly autobiographical. Maybe Dylan's best album ever and certainly one of

Above: *Mentors Ramblin' Jack Elliott, far left, and Dave Van Ronk, far right, with Dylan at the 1974 Friends of Chile Concert.*

the best albums of the 1970s, *Blood on the Tracks* reminded everyone what a truly great artist Dylan was and continued a rich creative period for him that lasted for some time.

Blood on the Tracks was a clear signal that Dylan's days of hiding out in Woodstock with his family and generally lying low were long over and that the period he had just gone through of experimenting with different musical ideas was at an end for the time being. He had been living in the Village again with his family since the late 1960s but was becoming very visible. In 1975, just prior to the official June release of the double album *The Basement Tapes*, this visibility included performing with many musicians. Dylan rekindled old friendships with Bob Neuwirth, Ramblin' Jack Elliott, and others. Neuwirth also introduced him to some of the up-and-coming musicians on the scene. At clubs such as the new Bottom Line and the Bitter End, Dylan met artists such as Patti Smith and Tom Verlaine of Television, who eventually became part of the punk and new wave scene. He also met Mick Ronson, T-Bone Burnett, and three artists who would appear with him on an upcoming television show.

Those three musicians, Howie Wyeth, Rob Stoner, and Scarlet Rivera, appeared with Dylan that September at a tribute to John Hammond, Sr., called "The World of John Hammond," as part of the PBS Soundstage series. The following month, while planning to record his *Desire* album, Dylan was inspired by Ramblin' Jack Elliott to embark on a very different kind of tour to support the album's release after it came out in December. Dylan turned to Neuwirth, who enlisted Stoner to put a band together that initially included Stoner, Howie Wyeth, Luther Rix, Mick Ronson, Scarlet Rivera, T-Bone Burnett, and David Mansfield. Subsequently added to the lineup were Roger McGuinn, Joan Baez, and, hot off her starring role in Robert Altman's landmark film *Nashville*, Ronee Blakely.

It soon became apparent that Dylan was looking to do more than just a tour. He was out to stage some kind of traveling hippie musical revue. This cosmic minstrel show took on an even more carnival-like atmosphere with the addition of several film crews, supervised by Howard Alk, who had worked on *Don't Look Back*. Rounding out this gypsy caravan were Allen Ginsberg, Peter Orlovsky, and David Blue, and at a show on October 23 at Manhattan's Folk City, just before the troupe set off on tour, Phil Ochs, Commander Cody and members of his Lost Planet Airmen, Bette Midler, and Buzzy Linhart joined in. Not all of the musicians made it to all the shows on the upcoming tour, which became known as the Rolling Thunder Revue. In fact, some never even made it beyond the Folk City sendoff/birthday party for the club's owner, Mike Porco.

On October 27, during the recording of *Desire*, Dylan's traveling hippie show set off for Plymouth, Massachusetts. The idea of the tour was to just show up in small New England towns, play small to mid-size venues, and keep

ticket prices to around $8 apiece. Dylan and many members of the entourage brought along their families, and this added to the familial spirit of the tour. Dylan's desire to do such a tour was both a reaction against the big rock tours that were becoming standard operating procedure and a need to reconnect to the spirit of the 1960s. Having along Ginsberg, Elliott, and Baez was symbolic of Dylan's sense of trying to understand his past and wanting to reconnect to the people who were so instrumental in shaping his early days.

Above: *Flyer for the Rolling Thunder Revue tour.*

Most of the shows were more than three hours long and gave all the participants a chance to bask in the spotlight. The feeling of everyone's being a part of the show was paramount to Dylan, and the openness of the entire enterprise encouraged even more musicians to join in along the way, such as Mimi Baez, Arlo Guthrie, Gordon Lightfoot, Robbie Robertson, Roberta Flack, and Eric Anderson.

Part of the perceived rebirth for Dylan came about as a result of his becoming involved in the plight of middleweight championship boxing contender Rubin "Hurricane" Carter. Dylan took on Carter's cause soon after the black fighter sent Dylan his autobiography, *The Sixteenth Round*, in the summer of 1975. Dylan learned of Carter's incarceration in a New Jersey jail for a triple murder that he and another man, John Artis, had allegedly committed.

Pages 76-77: *Dylan at a benefit concert for Rubin "Hurricane" Carter, flanked by Joan Baez, Allen Ginsberg, and Roberta Flack.*
Above: *(from left): Richie Havens, Joan Baez, Ramblin' Jack Elliott, Dylan, and others at a benefit for Rubin "Hurricane" Carter in 1975.*

Carter had been in jail since 1966 and was serving a life sentence. The two had been convicted of killing a bartender and two other men primarily on the testimony of Alfred Bello and Arthur Bradley, who both reportedly said they saw Carter and Artis running away from the bar after the shooting. In 1974 Bello and Bradley were reportedly overheard by a reporter for *The New York Times* and a private investigator saying that they had lied to the police about Carter and Artis in order to get help with cases pending against them for smaller crimes they had committed.

Carter's was an important cause to Dylan. Dylan had long written about the injustices of racism, and the writing of the song "Hurricane" (which was included on *Desire* and which became a big hit) was Dylan's first attempt at writing about such issues since "George Jackson." Dylan cowrote the lyrics of the song with Jacques Levy. Levy, who had cowritten the lyrics to all the songs on *Desire* except "Sara" and "Valley Below," held a Ph.D. in psychology and was a theater director who wrote many songs with Roger McGuinn, most notably "Chestnut Mare."

Dylan's involvement with Carter's plight helped bring about a New Jersey Supreme Court verdict in January 1976. The court overturned the earlier convictions of Carter and Artis. Both were released on bail and promised a new trial. Regardless of the suspected racism and false testimony of the earlier trial, a second trial also found them guilty. However, in November 1985 Carter was finally released, again on bail, by a federal judge.

Dylan's help on Carter's behalf went beyond the writing of "Hurricane." There were two benefit shows at the end of the Rolling Thunder Revue. The Night of the Hurricane I was held at Madison Square Garden in New York

City on December 8, 1975, and was a star-studded event that included Mohammed Ali and then-future President Jimmy Carter. A second show, the Night of the Hurricane II, held at the Houston Astrodome on January 25, 1976, featured Stevie Wonder, Steve Stills, Ringo Starr, Dr. John, Santana, Shawn Phillips, and Isaac Hayes, but was not considered very successful in that only thirty thousand tickets were sold.

Columbia released *Desire* in January 1976. With the single "Hurricane" zooming up the charts, Dylan's new sound was clearly a lot looser and filled with a varied instrumental backing. *Blood on the Tracks* was an intense, personal, carefully constructed album; *Desire* was something completely different.

Including many of the same musicians from the Rolling Thunder Revue and with vocals shared on many of the cuts by Emmylou Harris, *Desire* is one of Dylan's most passionate and musical albums. Scarlet Rivera's careening gypsy violin pierces the music with exuberant abandon, and world music rhythms enliven the jaunty "Mozambique." "Hurricane," "Mozambique," "Isis," "Black Diamond Bay," and "Sara" filled the FM and, in some cases, AM airwaves for months. "Sara," with it's lyrics "Stayin' up for days in the Chelsea Hotel/Writin' 'Sad-Eyed Lady of the Lowlands' for you," is Dylan's most autobiographical family song.

Desire was replete with beautiful music, including "One More Cup of Coffee," "Oh Sister," and, perhaps recalling his work on *Pat Garrett*, "Romance in Durango." The album is a spicy, confident, uninhibited work that gives some indication of the sound Dylan undertook on his next studio album. (Unfortunately, fans had to wait three years for that.)

In September 1976 Dylan released his second official live album, *Hard Rain*, taken from an NBC television broadcast of a concert performance the previous May at Hughes Stadium in Fort Collins, Colorado. The album leaned heavily on songs from *Blood on the Tracks* and *Desire*, and was met with mixed reaction. What was clear, though, was how the concert did not bring to the screen any of the magic of the Rolling Thunder Revue. That could have been achieved by a release instead of footage from any of the intimate, seminal club shows or the late fall concert-hall leg of the tour.

Dylan's next big appearance almost didn't happen. The Band decided to retire from the road and put on a big concert in San Francisco with many guests that was released as a film called *The Last Waltz*. The concert was staged at Winterland and filmed by acclaimed director Martin Scorsese. With the Berkeley Promenade Orchestra providing music to waltz by, the five thousand in attendance spent Thanksgiving of 1976 satisfying their munchies with turkey and salmon. The

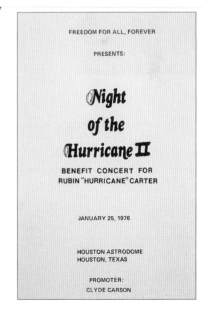

FREEDOM FOR ALL, FOREVER

PRESENTS:

Night of the Hurricane II

BENEFIT CONCERT FOR
RUBIN "HURRICANE" CARTER

JANUARY 25, 1976

HOUSTON ASTRODOME
HOUSTON, TEXAS

PROMOTER:
CLYDE CARSON

Above left: *A rare cover for Dylan's double-sided single, "Hurricane."* **Above, center:** *A ticket stub from the Rolling Thunder Revue.* **Above right:** *A pamphlet for the poorly attended Night of the Hurricane II at the Houston Astrodome.*

stage sets were borrowed from the San Francisco Opera's *La Traviata* production. The host was novelist and former "digger" Emmett Grogan; San Francisco renaissance poets Lawrence Ferlinghetti, Michael McClure, and several others supplied readings from their poems. Scorcese scripted the entire shoot, with seven cameras and a crew of forty-five. The cinematographers on the project were Laszlo Kovacs and Vilmos Zsigmond. Many regard it as the best film about rock ever produced, even to this day.

Ironically, the shooting of the film was the number one reason Dylan almost never appeared. The mercurial Dylan most likely wanted to pay homage to his first real band on their farewell to touring, but ever careful to control his own image, he did not want to be filmed. Even minutes before his appearance, the order was not to film him—but of course he was filmed and he stole the show. The film and soundtrack album, both released in 1978, further proved the electricity that Dylan and The Band still had.

The following year, 1977, was a relatively quiet one for Dylan. In 1978 there was more touring, and *At Budokan*, a live double album, was released only in Japan. (The stateside release came a year later.) While in the past Dylan had been known to rearrange his songs somewhat, the arrangements of his old songs on this Budokan tour were almost unrecognizable until many verses along in a given song. Such dramatic reworking of his old songs continues right up to today and is still met rather unhappily by many of Dylan's fans.

Early 1978 also saw the first reviews of Dylan's film *Renaldo and Clara* appear after its January release. Combining more than one hundred hours of film of concerts, backstage footage, and dramatic fiction set pieces, the film was originally released at four hours in length. Later, some two-hour cuts were screened. The reaction by U.S. critics was almost unanimously negative. Many felt the film was self-indulgent, and the scenes that featured Dylan, his wife, and Joan Baez made people downright uncomfortable because of the sexual tension between Dylan and Baez. Critics in Europe were a little more open-minded, and some actually thought the film was one of the best of the year.

American playwright Sam Shepard, who had been recruited to write a script for *Renaldo and Clara*, detailed the making of the film and the Rolling Thunder Revue tour itself in his must-read book *Rolling Thunder Logbook*. He never did write a script for the film, and all the dramatic sequences were totally improvised. The movie came at a time when American films had become completely free of the old studio system and directors such as Scorcese, Francis Ford Coppola, Robert Altman, and others were making American films in the European auteur tradition. Dylan admitted how the French new wave films were partly a model for *Renaldo and Clara*, and the climate was right for the kind of experimental film Dylan envisioned. The reaction of critics, however, kept Dylan away from films for many years.

Left: *Dylan, with Robbie Robertson of The Band, at The Last Waltz.*

Above: *British fans await Dylan in a hard rain at Earls Court.*

Above: *A scene from Dylan's film,* Renaldo and Clara.

CHAPTER SIX

Knockin' On Heaven's Door

Opposite: *Dylan during the* Street Legal *tour in 1978.* Street Legal *marked Dylan's conversion to a born-again Christian.*
Above: *Dylan on tour, 1978.*

Thunder Revue, would sometimes paint his face white and wear eye makeup while playing live. He was attempting to bring visual artistic touches to his performances and to create a stage show vastly different from his earlier, rather no-frills style. He had been successfully painting Picassoesque art for years, and of course his original works had been integral to the presentation of *Self Portrait* and *Planet Waves*. Also noteworthy is the fine illustration he did for the cover of The Band's *Music from Big Pink*. This visual approach to his music is clear in such songs on *Street Legal* as the brilliant "Señor (Tales of Yankee Power)" and "Where Are You Tonight (Journey Through Dark Heat)." These songs are like mini movies, as the lyrics conjure up vivid images like a film, and though the critics thought he was unsuccessful with *Renaldo and Clara*, his film experience did bring a heightened visual quality to his music that worked. On "Señor" the creative writing process was again something Dylan had a hard time figuring, as he stated in the *Biograph* notes: "Sometimes you'll write something because you've lived something and you someplace along the line say to yourself, 'Why am I writing this? It will never be as good as I lived it.' But then it sometimes turns out better than what you've lived....In some kind of way I see this as the aftermath of when two people who were leaning on each other because neither one of them had the guts to stand alone, all of a sudden they break apart....I think I felt that way when I wrote it."

Once again, the critics confused some of Dylan's musical ideas on the album and onstage. His larger group and his sometimes dressing in a suit that subtly recalled an Elvis outfit brought cries of Dylan going Vegas. What was actually happening was that Dylan was bringing his love of gospel to his sound and his performances. *Street Legal* was produced by Columbia house producer Don DeVito. The most distinct change in the music was the addition of background singers Carolyn Dennis, Jo Ann Harris, and Helena Springs. On such songs as "Changing of the Guard" and "New Pony" they brought a decidedly gospel-like, tent-revival feel and served as the perfect counterpoint to Dylan's impassioned R&B/soul/gospel vocalizing.

Dylan was living most of the time at his large house in Malibu and dating actress Mary Alice Artes, who is listed on the back cover notes of *Street Legal* as Queen Bee. Artes is widely believed to have influenced Dylan to become a born-again Christian. How true this is is hard to say. Dylan has over the years alternately shunned and embraced his Jewish background. His music has always been filled with religious imagery, particularly biblical references, and of course he is a seeker. He has always made it clear that he doesn't offer answers in his music. His arrival at religious rapture has been discussed in numerous articles, papers, and books, and like any number of other seemingly incongruous steps along his path of life, this was met with scorn and resistance.

With *Renaldo and Clara*, the Rolling Thunder Revue, and his marriage to Sara behind him, a big tour was scheduled for Dylan. His next album, *Street Legal*, released in 1978, was an important transitional work. With a tour imminent, the album was quickly recorded at Rundown Studios in Santa Monica in April and dedicated to Emmett Grogan; in retrospect, it is a very strong Dylan album. The effects of *Renaldo and Clara* were still evident. Dylan continued to use subtle stage costumes and, as with the Rolling

Above: *Dylan having a little fun during a soundcheck.*

Dylan began his life as a Christian in 1978 at the home of pastor Bill Dwyer, where he was baptized as part of the Vineyard Fellowship, based in Tarzana, California. He then enrolled in the School of Discipleship, where he studied the Bible five days a week for more than three months. The musical result of this complete religious conversion was 1979's *Slow Train Coming*, easily one of his most satisfying musical albums, for himself as well as for his fans.

The songs on the album were also apparently influenced by Hal Lindsey's book *The Late Great Planet Earth*. Again, it is interesting that fans and critics seemed so shocked that Dylan would be so interested in this kind of thought when his music had been filled with biblical imagery and apocalyptic signs since his early days.

Slow Train Coming was recorded in April at the famed Muscle Shoals Sound Studio in Muscle Shoals, Alabama. It was produced by Jerry Wexler and Barry Beckett, veteran producers of American R&B who produced such Atlantic Records artists as Ray Charles and Aretha Franklin, and it featured such musicians as drummer Pick Withers and lead guitarist and principal

Above: *The weary troubadour.*

songwriter Mark Knopfler, the vocalist of Dire Straits. Joining Dylan on vocals for the sessions were Dennis and Springs from the *Street Legal* recordings, this time with Regina Havis. With Beckett on keyboards, the rhythm section was rounded out by Tim Drummond.

It's interesting that Dylan, who was looking for a raw gospel sound and who chose the swampy environs of Alabama as the place to record the album, came up with one of his cleanest and most measured recordings, which also incorporated some of his most pronounced vocalizing. The centerpiece track of the album was the opening cut, "Gotta Serve Somebody," about which Dylan said on the sleeve notes to *Biograph*, "I had to fight to get it on the album; it was ridiculous." In the lyrics Dylan basically states that a person can serve himself, his demons, sin, the devil, or the Lord. The song is also the only one on the album where Dylan brings a little humor to the proceedings with the lines "You may call me Terry, you may call me Timmy/You may call me Bobby, you may call me Zimmy/You may call me R.J., you may call me Ray/You may call me anything but no matter what you say/You're gonna have to serve somebody, yes indeed."

In support of the album, which came out that August, Dylan made a rare live television appearance in October on *Saturday Night Live*, performing "Gotta Serve Somebody," "I Believe in You," and "When You Gonna Wake Up." (In February 1980, Dylan performed "Gotta Serve Somebody." at the Grammy Awards, and *Slow Train Coming* won in the Best Male Rock Vocal category, earning Dylan his first Grammy.)

Live performances supporting the album during November and December 1979, beginning in San Francisco and moving through Arizona and New Mexico, were filled almost exclusively with Dylan's new Christian music. The tour opened with fourteen nights of inspired performances at San Francisco's Fox-Warfield Theater, featuring only the new music. In addition to the fact that Dylan wouldn't play any of his older material, he also alienated the audiences by delivering long sermons from the stage challenging his audience to get with the Lord.

With an upcoming tour for which he would not perform any older material, Dylan began writing songs that he felt would both reflect his then-current religious feelings and sound good live. These were songs that appeared on his next album, *Saved*. On the sleeve notes to *Biograph*, Dylan explained how some of this music was perceived: " 'In the Garden' and 'Solid Rock' kind of went by everybody like all my stuff at a certain time, maybe people need time to catch up with it, I don't know. I was suffering that so-called religious backlash at the time and that had a lot to do with affecting people's opinions. I think people were prejudiced against it."

Right: *Dylan on the* Street Legal *tour.*

Dylan returned to Muscle Shoals in February 1980 to record *Saved*. Again Dylan chose bassist Tim Drummond, but this time Drummond was paired with famed drummer Jim Keltner, which gave the music an even bigger backbeat than that on *Slow Train Coming*. Rounding out this killer lineup was guitarist Fred Tackett and keyboardist Spooner Oldham. Regina Havis rejoined Dylan on vocals, and additional vocal support was provided by Clydie King, Mona Lisa Young, and Terry Young, who also played keyboards. The album, released that June, includes a cover of Red Hayes and Jack Rhodes' "A Satisfied Mind." The title track was cowritten by Dylan and Drummond. With Wexler and Beckett back behind the controls, the album, though not quite as strong as *Slow Train Coming*, offered some super playing. "Solid Rock" foreshadowed the exuberance and passion that exploded on Dylan's next album.

In 1981, *Shot of Love*, the final album in Dylan's trilogy of what has been called his Christian period, was released. Dylan coproduced the album with Chuck Plotkin. Plotkin had been working in the studio with Bruce Springsteen and went on to coproduce most of Springsteen's albums with Springsteen and his manager, Jon Landau. *Shot of Love*, however, is not made up exclusively of songs of Dylan's religious conversion, as evidenced by the brilliant "Lenny Bruce." It also includes another Dylan classic, "Every Grain of Sand," and the blistering title cut, the only song produced by Bumps Blackwell. The musical support throughout was inspired, with Keltner, Drummond, Tackett, and King returning from the *Saved* album, and with additional support supplied by a myriad of players, most notably keyboardist Benmont Tench from Tom Petty and the Heartbreakers (foreshadowing Dylan's eventual playing with that band), Danny Kortchmar, Ringo Starr, Donald "Duck" Dunn, and Ron Wood from the Rolling Stones. *Shot of Love* was quickly re-released with the song "The Groom's Still Waiting at the Altar," originally the U.S. B side of the single "Heart of Mine."

For *Shot of Love*, there were some songs written but not recorded, as well as songs recorded but never released, as is often the case with Dylan. In talking about the previously unreleased track "Caribbean Wind," which was recorded for the *Shot of Love* sessions but is included on the *Biograph* box set instead, Dylan gave some insight into his songwriting: "That one I couldn't quite grasp what it was about after I finished it. Sometimes you'll write something to be very inspired, and you won't quite finish it for one reason or another. Then you'll go back and try and pick it up, and the inspiration is just gone. Either you get it all, and you can leave a few little pieces to fill in, or you're always trying to finish it off. Then it's a struggle. The inspiration's gone and you can't remember why you started it in the first place. Frustration sets in. I think there's four different sets of lyrics to this; maybe I got it right, I don't know. I had to leave it. I just dropped it. Sometimes that happens."

Opposite: *Dylan takes a break from the stage during the* Street Legal *tour.* **Right:** *Dylan performing with guitar in 1978.*

Dylan's bringing in Plotkin was a clear sign that he was not going to be relegated to the nostalgia bins in record stores. The 1980s were taking shape as a decade that would represent the complete opposite of much of what Dylan's music had stood for. With Ronald Reagan in the White House and hippies turned into Wall Street yuppies, America had become very conservative on the right; on the left, rather than long-haired, mellow acoustic guitar players, there now were the last remnants of punk rock morphing into new wave. Surprisingly, Dylan again entered a rich creative period and found other ways to bring his music to a public too old to have time for pop music anymore as well as to a younger crowd more interested in watching MTV.

CHAPTER SEVEN

Don't Look Back

Opposite: *Looking towards heaven's door.* **Above:** *Dylan poses for a portrait after being inducted into the Songwriters Hall of Fame.*

In 1982, Dylan was clearly keeping things in high gear and maintaining a very active schedule of writing, recording, and performing. While many other artists who first came to prominence in the 1960s were by this time forgotten, retired, resting on their laurels, joining the nostalgia circuit, or releasing relatively uninspired albums every three to five years, Dylan remained as active, fresh, and relevant as ever.

Reviewing the available information on songs written by Dylan and on those he covered either live or in the studio, as well as on recordings of his own songs never released up to this point, is daunting. Dylan's continued ability to write songs and his love of covering other artists' songs, particularly from old rock, country, and blues, illustrate his innate drive, compositional prowess, and outright love of just picking up a guitar and playing.

Early 1982 saw Dylan writing and recording in collaboration with poet Allen Ginsberg, whom Dylan had long admired. In March Dylan was inducted into the prestigious Songwriters Hall of Fame. During his brief speech when he accepted the award, he quipped, "I think this is pretty amazing really, because I can't read or write a note of music."

On June 6 he joined Joan Baez yet again, performing at Peace Sunday, a concert and rally in support of the United Nations' Special Session on Nuclear Disarmament. The event was organized by Baez and held at the Rose Bowl in Pasadena, California. Dylan sang with Baez, performing "With God on Our Side," "Blowin' in the Wind," and Jimmy Buffet's "A Pirate Looks at Forty."

Further solidifying his obvious attempt to have his music reach as many people as possible, in August he hired Elliot Roberts to be his manager. Roberts had come up the rock management ladder with David Geffen and over the years has been a manager for many artists, including Joni Mitchell and Neil Young.

In 1983 Dylan began recording *Infidels*, one of his finest post–*Blood on the Tracks* albums, at the Power Station in Manhattan. Because of his work with Dylan over the previous few years, Dire Straits frontman Mark Knopfler was asked to produce the album. Having already worked with many great backing bands live and in the studio, Dylan came up with a lineup that seemed unbeatable. Two reggae artists, drummer Sly Dunbar and bassist Robbie Shakespeare, were recruited as the rhythm section. Along with guitarist Knopfler, Dire Straits' Alan Clark joined on keyboards, and rounding out the lineup was Mick Taylor, who after leaving John Mayall's Bluesbreakers is best known as the man who replaced Brian Jones in the Rolling Stones. With Neil Dorfsman recording everything, Josh Abbey engineering, and Ian Taylor doing the mixing, *Infidels* was one of Dylan's finest releases. The songs on the album were clearly inspired by the geopolitical makeup of the early 1980s, such as "Man of Peace," "License to Kill," and "Jokerman." "Neighborhood Bully" could have been about such despised world leaders as Mu'ammar Gadhafi, Manuel Noriega, and Saddam Hussein.

On "Union Sundown," Dylan talks about the export of cheap labor around the world and the loss of blue collar jobs by Americans. "Sweetheart Like You" is on the surface a love song, but with the lines "They say that patriotism is the last refuge/To which a scoundrel clings/Steal a little and they throw you in jail/Steal a lot and they make you king," it prefigures the fallout of the 1980s Wall Street greed machine. Compositionally, it is to Dylan's credit as a writer and vocalist that he is able to take clichéd song titles and lyrics and make them all his own while creating something with profound meaning.

Infidels was released in November, and after some apparent conflict between Dylan and Knopfler during the recording process, Dylan did extensive

Above: *Dylan strikes a pose for a cover shoot for his 1985 album,* Empire Burlesque.

re-recording and overdubbing, and made other major changes that perhaps took something away from the final product. Many have speculated that if Dylan hadn't tinkered with the recording so much, the final album, outstanding as it is on its own merits, would have been one of Dylan's post–1960s masterpieces.

Dylan began 1984 with some very public performances. He appeared at the 1984 Grammy Awards, presenting an award with Stevie Wonder. In March he performed on David Letterman's *Late Night* television show on NBC, after which the host asked him if he'd like to come back and perform every Thursday night.

Dylan continued to write songs at a breakneck pace. He went on a barnstorming tour through Europe from May to July. He also did lots of recording at various locations with many different supporting musicians. As the year came to a close, he spent a considerable amount of time working on a long song, one of his most ambitious, cowritten with Sam Shepard. Initially called "New Danville Girl," the song became "Brownsville Girl" and was released on 1986's *Knocked Out Loaded*. In December he released *Real Live*, his fourth live album. The musicians included the rhythm section of bassist Greg Sutton, drummer Colin Allen, and former Faces keyboardist Ian McLagen, as well as Mick Taylor on guitar. Produced by veteran British producer Glyn Johns, who has worked with the Who, the Rolling Stones, and the Eagles, the album is made up mostly of Dylan's 1960s classics (including "Tombstone Blues," on which Carlos Santana adds guitar), with "Tangled Up in Blue" and two songs from *Infidels*, "License to Kill" and "I and I," also included.

In early 1985 Dylan recorded with three members of Tom Petty's Heartbreakers: keyboardist Benmont Tench, guitarist Mike Campbell, and the newest Heartbreaker, bassist Howie Epstein. On the night of January 28 and into the next morning, Dylan participated in the recording of U.S.A. for Africa's "We Are the World," the response by American artists to Bob Geldof's having arranged the recording of Band Aid's "Do They Know It's Christmas" in England the previous year. Both recordings raised money to feed starving children in Africa.

In February, after several months of recording, Dylan began wrapping up the recording of *Empire Burlesque*. In March he brought in rap and hip-hop producer Arthur Baker to mix the album. Although Baker's touch did add a modern edge with fine results on songs like "Tight Connection to My Heart" and "When the Night Comes Falling from the Sky," for the most part his contribution came across as ham-handed. Songs like "Clean Cut Kid" and "Dark Eyes," which appeared to have the least Baker intervention, were pure Dylan. The album was finally released in June.

In July Dylan began rehearsing with Ron Wood and Keith Richards for Live Aid, which organized concerts in England and America to raise money for

Above: *Dylan performing at Wembley Stadium in England, July 1984.*

starving children in Africa. Dylan was the last artist to perform at the event, held on July 13 at JFK Stadium in Philadelphia, before the all-star finale. With Wood and Richards he performed "Ballad of Hollis Brown"; "When the Ship Comes In," which he hadn't played live in years; and "Blowin' in the Wind." Due to obstructed stage monitors and the less than enthusiastic response by the crowd following the preceding high-energy performances, Dylan's performance was not considered one of his best for such a major event. However, he made comments from the stage about how Americans must also work to take care of problems at home, and he mentioned America's farmers. His comments prompted Willie Nelson to organize Farm Aid.

The Farm Aid concerts were held at Memorial Stadium in Champaign, Illinois, on September 22. In addition to Dylan's being the impetus for the event and bringing his name and performance to it, Farm Aid marked an important musical crossroads for Dylan. Any time over the years that Dylan was not playing with The Band, he was supported by excellent musicians. His ability both to play with well-known artists who could easily have their own bands and to spot bright new musicians has always been uncanny; yet having the backing of a self-contained unit other than The Band had eluded him. At Farm Aid, he got the first taste of playing with the only other group that would afford him the kind of band unity he had enjoyed with The Band: Tom Petty and the Heartbreakers.

Tom Petty and the Heartbreakers had emerged around the time of the first punk arrival in the mid-1970s. Though they hailed from Florida, they were actually mistaken for a British band by many. By the time they played with Dylan, they had firmly established themselves as one of American rock's premier groups. Their sound had the grit of the Rolling Stones with the twang of the Byrds. In fact, their song "American Girl" had been performed by Roger McGuinn, making for an early Dylan connection.

Dylan and the group rehearsed extensively for Farm Aid and performed six songs together, unannounced: "Clean Cut Kid," something loosely called "Shake," "I'll Remember You," "Trust Yourself," "That Lucky Ol' Sun," and (with Nelson joining in) "Maggie's Farm." Their excellent performance proved that the pairing was a perfect fit. Like Dylan, Tom Petty and the Heartbreakers had an encyclopedic knowledge of so much music other than their own, as well as an affinity for playing it, that their sensibilities were perfectly matched with Dylan's to create great rock and roll. Fortunately, this charity event was not the last time these musicians played together.

In October Dylan was involved in another musical project geared to raise consciousness. In South Africa, amid apartheid, a resort called Sun City played host to some of the biggest names in entertainment. Steve Van Zandt, of Bruce Springsteen's band, organized the recording of a song called "Sun City," which

Left: *Ron Wood, Bob Dylan, and Keith Richards at Live Aid on July 13, 1985, at JFK Stadium in Philadelphia, Pennsylvania.*

Above: *Future Wilbury brothers, Bob Dylan and Tom Petty.*

in no uncertain terms called for all musicians to refuse to play in South Africa as long as apartheid existed. Both the song and its video included Dylan. These events—Live Aid, Farm Aid, and Sun City—were the kind of politically and socially conscious events for which Dylan's career had stood. In the face of the "greeding" frenzy of Ronald Reagan's 1980s America, they were a reminder of the power of music to bring about change.

That year closed with projects and events that celebrated Dylan's long career, revived his name in the publishing world, and brought out lots of unreleased material. In November Knopf published *Lyrics 1962–1985*, which was an update of Dylan's 1973 book, *Writings and Drawings*. Also in November, CBS Records held a tribute to Dylan at the Whitney Museum in New York that marked his having sold thirty-five million records. On hand to pay tribute to him were Pete Townshend, David Bowie, Dave Stewart, Neil Young, and

Billy Joel. The big event of 1985 for Dylan fans, though, occurred in October with the release of *Biograph*. With lots of music being reissued on compact disc, the music of Bob Dylan had to be at the top of any record label's list of artists most deserving of careful reissue.

Biograph was released as a five-album or three-CD set and featured twenty-two tracks that had not previously appeared on other albums. Some of the highlights of the unreleased material included "I'll Keep It with Mine," "Mixed-Up Confusion," "Lay Down Your Weary Tune," a live version of "Visions of Johanna," and "Quinn the Eskimo," which was recorded at the *Basement Tapes* sessions.

"Lay Down Your Weary Tune" was originally recorded in New York City in October 1963. Dylan's recollection on writing it reveals his way of deriving inspiration while carrying on the folk songwriting process: "I wrote that on the

Above: *Elizabeth Taylor, left, in 1986 at a television appearance with Dylan.*

Australia, they recorded a song called "Band of the Hand" for a film of the same name.

That April Dylan had a screen test for and landed a role in a film called *Hearts of Fire*, directed by Richard Marquand, who also directed such films as *Eye of the Needle*, *Return of the Jedi*, and *Jagged Edge*. Marquand died in 1987 at the age of forty-nine, before *Hearts of Fire* was released. In the film, Dylan played the part of a fictitious musician named Billy Parker. The film was poorly received and had no U.S. theatrical release.

At the end of April and into May, Dylan again attempted to record with the Heartbreakers, but did not appear to have the right material to put an album together. Petty and Dylan did write a song called "Jammin' Me," which was further developed by Mike Campbell and which appeared as the first single off the future Tom Petty and the Heartbreakers album *Let Me Up (I've Had Enough)*. Also in May, Dylan recorded several tracks with other musicians that appeared on *Knocked Out Loaded*. Closing out a busy month, Dylan rejoined Petty and the Heartbreakers at Zoetrope Studios in Hollywood, California, to rehearse for their upcoming tour.

Dylan and the group began the tour on June 9 at the Sports Arena in San Diego, California. The American dates also featured two sets with just Petty and the Heartbreakers, unlike their previous shows with Dylan. Soon after, a film called *Hard to Handle*, which featured one of the Sydney shows, was shown on HBO and later released on video.

That August, *Knocked Out Loaded* was released. The album featured some of the Heartbreakers on "Maybe Someday" and "Got My Mind Made Up" (written by Dylan and Petty). There is a long list of folks thanked on the album (a record for a Dylan album), including Jack Nicholson, Harry Dean Stanton, Martin Sheen, Ronnie Spector, Alan Rudolph, and unidentified friends like Girl Shaped Like a Frog. Also thanked was Carole Childs, an A&R representative for Elektra Records rumored to be Dylan's longtime girlfriend. The highlights of the album are "Brownsville Girl" and a cover of Kris Kristofferson's chilling "They Killed Him." Written with Sam Shepard, "Brownsville Girl" is an epic film on record that was partially inspired by the Gregory Peck film *The Gunfighter*.

Demonstrating his admiration for Gordon Lightfoot, Dylan inducted Lightfoot into the Juno Hall of Fame on November 10. (The Juno is the Canadian version of the Grammy.) In regard to how Dylan felt about Lightfoot (one of the few contemporary artists about whom he had anything to say in the *Biograph* booklet), Dylan said, "Every time I hear a song of his, it's like I wish it would last forever."

Early 1987 saw Dylan drop in on the Grateful Dead while they were recording in Marin County, California. Dylan sang "Soon" at a tribute to

West Coast, at Joan Baez's house. She had a place outside Big Sur. I had heard a Scottish ballad on an old 78 record that I was trying to really capture the feeling of, that was haunting me. I couldn't get it out of my head. There were no lyrics or anything; it was just a melody, had bagpipes and a lot of stuff in it. I wanted lyrics that would feel the same way. I don't remember what the original record was, but this was pretty similar to that—the melody anyway." *Biograph* proved that music buyers were willing to plunk down big bucks for multidisc sets with lots of unreleased tracks.

Without missing a beat, the promise of Farm Aid led to a full-scale tour with Dylan backed by Tom Petty and the Heartbreakers. Dylan and the group began rehearsals in December at Universal Studios' Soundstage 41. They then embarked on a tour, playing the first show at Athletic Park in Wellington, New Zealand, on February 5, 1986. Right around that time, in Sydney,

Above: Dylan rehearsing in March of 1987 for a George Gershwin tribute at the Brooklyn Academy of Music.

George Gershwin at the Brooklyn Academy of Music in March that marked the fiftieth anniversary of the composer's death. Shortly thereafter, in April, Dylan began sessions for what became *Down in the Groove*. Much like the often maligned *Self Portrait*, this is an album of mostly covers; it does, however, contain three Dylan compositions—his own arrangement of "Shenandoah" and two songs he cowrote with Grateful Dead lyricist Robert Hunter, "Ugliest Girl in the World" and the very memorable "Silvio." In June, the visit that Dylan had made to the Dead's recording sessions in the earlier part of the year turned into rehearsals with the group for a tour. Dylan and the Dead performed six shows together, opening on July 4 at Sullivan Stadium in Foxborough, Massachusetts, and continued on to Philadelphia, New Jersey; and West Coast dates in Eugene, Oregon, and Oakland and Anaheim, California.

Above: *In 1988, Dylan and the Grateful Dead released a live album of their brief 1987 summer tour.*

Although some questioned Dylan's decision to play in front of devoted Deadheads, the pairing made perfect musical sense. Both Dylan and the Dead have always been live performers more than recording artists. Both also have an affinity for improvisation and varying set lists from night to night. Above all, both Dylan and the Dead are musicians first and everything else second, and bring to their respective musical sounds years and years of mixing myriad musical styles and genres from many eras. The respect these artists have for the art form of popular music is without question, and maybe with some more rehearsal time and shows performed at more intimate venues, the tour may have been more memorable.

Throughout September and October, Dylan rejoined Tom Petty and the Heartbreakers for a tour in Israel and Europe. On October 9, *Hearts of Fire* was released, along with a soundtrack album—neither of which was commercially or critically successful. Dylan closed the year by recording "Pretty Boy Floyd" for *Folkways: A Vision Shared*, a tribute to Woody Guthrie and Leadbelly that was released in August 1988.

In January 1988, Dylan was inducted into the Rock and Roll Hall of Fame by Bruce Springsteen. In his sincere, eloquent speech, Springsteen perhaps best summed up Dylan's enormous influence when he said, "Dylan was a revolutionary. Bob freed the mind the way Elvis freed the body. He showed us that just because the music was innately physical did not mean that it was anti-intellectual. He had the vision and the talent to make a pop song that con-

tained the whole world. He invented a new way a pop singer could sound, broke through the limitations of what a recording artist could achieve, and changed the face of rock and roll forever."

An April phone call from George Harrison led to the birth of one of the most super supergroups of all time. Harrison had just wrapped up the recording of *Cloud Nine*, his first album in years, and was looking to record a quick B side for the single in Europe. He called Dylan and asked if he could use the studio in Dylan's garage in Malibu. Harrison brought Jeff Lynne along to coproduce and Lynne brought along Roy Orbison, whom he was producing. On the ride over they stopped at Tom Petty's house to pick up a guitar and Petty decided to go with them. When this fab four showed up, Dylan decided to join in on the recording; the resulting song, "Handle with Care," was so strong that they all agreed to record an album in May. Recording at Dave Stewart's Los Angeles studio with Jim Keltner brought in on drums, the group, under the moniker the Traveling Wilburys, recorded nine songs in ten days. Three songs primarily penned by Dylan—"Dirty World," "Congratulations," and "Tweeter and the Monkey Man"—and "Handle with Care" were the highlights. "Tweeter and the Monkey Man" has a slight Springsteen feel (with tongue planted firmly in cheek) and reminded folks that Dylan did indeed have quite a sense of humor. Needless to say, the Traveling Wilburys were one of the most pleasant musical surprises of the year. *Traveling Wilburys, Volume 1.* was released to great critical and commercial acclaim in mid-October. Sadly, on December 7, less than two months after the record's release, Roy Orbison died of a heart attack in Nashville, Tennessee.

Above left: *Along with Judy Collins, Richie Havens (far left) has been and still is one of the best interpreters of Dylan's songs.*
Above right: *George Harrison and Bob Dylan were inducted into the Rock and Roll Hall of Fame in January 1988.*

Above: *Dylan flanked by Bruce Springsteen and Mick Jagger at the Rock and Roll Hall of Fame induction jam in 1988.*

CHAPTER EIGHT

Oh Mercy

Opposite: *Dylan at the February 1991 Grammy Awards, where he was awarded a Lifetime Achievement award, presented by fellow iconoclast Jack Nicholson.* **Above:** *Dylan at "Bobfest."*

big way. In fact, a host of singer-songwriters with roots in folk were coming up with a sound that brought to music a real sincerity, which had been sorely lacking in much of the music of the video-age 1980s. There was a hunger again for the kind of spiritual awakening that had happened in the 1960s, evident in the further growth in the popularity of new age philosophies.

Looking back on the 1960s, in the booklet for *Biograph*, Dylan said: "People who were in it [the 1960s], it never occurred to anybody that they were living in the sixties. It was too much of a pressure cooker. There wasn't any time to sit around and think about it....People like to think of themselves as being important when they write about things that are important....It was like a flying saucer landed....that's what the sixties were like. Everybody heard about it, but only a few really saw it."

Sometime during the summer of 1988, Dylan played some of the new songs that he was working on for Bono of U2. Bono suggested that Dylan get Daniel Lanois to produce them. Lanois was a Canadian who had worked with Brian Eno on some of his ambient recordings, and had gone on to produce U2, the Neville Brothers, and Robbie Robertson. Bono's suggestion proved fortuitous.

On February 6, 1989, *Dylan & the Dead* was released. Coproduced by Jerry Garcia and John Cutler, recorded using the Dead's mobile studio, and complete with psychedelic cover art by Rick Griffin, the album documents the best of the six shows recorded in 1988. Aside from "Joey," the album is short on the kind of improvising one would expect from Dylan and the Grateful Dead. The inclusion of "Queen Jane Approximately," however, was warmly greeted by those who had rarely heard Dylan perform the song live.

In March, Dylan began recording *Oh Mercy*, which Lanois produced with assistance by Malcolm Burn. The recordings were done at two separate locations in New Orleans using Lanois' Studio on the Move, a mobile recording studio. With musical support by Mason Ruffner, Cyril Neville, Rockin' Dopsie, Willie Green, Lanois, and Burn, among others, Lanois was able to bring out the best in Dylan.

Finished in May, the album has the same kind of atmospheric soundscape for which Lanois was becoming known. Dylan's vocal performance is superb, with a breathy, whispery style on the album's two best tracks, "Man in the Long Black Coat" and "Most of the Time." On "Everything Is Broken," there is a vocal phrasing by Dylan in which he almost seems to parody himself, but the track works well and is almost danceable. There are also two songs that brought about the best recent covers of Dylan's songs: "Ring Them Bells," covered by Gordon Lightfoot on his 1993 release, *Waiting for You*, and "What Was It You Wanted," masterfully done by blues-folk veteran Chris Smither on his

As the 1980s drew to a close, the United States was beginning to reap what it had sown. The Wall Street semicrash of October 1987 had proven that the junk bond–fueled stock market was in many ways a house of cards. Ronald Reagan's economic policies had made the rich richer and the poor poorer and accelerated the shrinking of the middle class. His foreign policy, mostly via the unraveling of the Iran-Contra scandal, had brought back shades of Nixon. The 1960s were revisited with the celebration of the twentieth anniversary of the "Summer of Love" and the reissue of *Sgt. Pepper's Lonely Hearts Club Band* in 1987, as well as the twentieth anniversary of the Woodstock festival in 1989. Classic rock radio was also breathing new life into the old sounds, while new artists like Tracy Chapman were bringing social concerns back into music in a

Above left: *Carlos Santana has toured with Dylan on many occasions over the years.*

1995 album, *Up on the Lowdown*. These versions of Dylan's songs prove that he could still write new material that resonated with sympathetic interpreters.

In June, Dylan continued what has come to be known as the Never Ending Tour, which continued his never-ending lineup change. He also performed with Van Morrison for a television special he was taping in Greece that month, which was broadcast the following March.

Oh Mercy was released on September 22, and of course, the critical hosannas began flying. Dylan proved that if he was patient in the studio and worked with the right producer, he could still come up with a great album. He continued to tour extensively, and a long stint at Manhattan's Beacon Theatre gave him a chance to showcase his new album.

In January 1990, Dylan began recording songs for his next album with producers David and Don Was and Jack Frost. Don had just come off a highly successful stint producing Bonnie Raitt's triumphant, Grammy Award–winning comeback album, *Nick of Time*.

Dylan continued to tour extensively, and on February 24 he made a surprise appearance at a tribute to Roy Orbison at the Universal Amphitheatre in Los Angeles. He joined three-fifths of the original Byrds—Roger McGuinn, Chris Hillman, and David Crosby—for a performance of "Mr. Tambourine Man" (which appeared on the Byrds' 1990 four-CD box set). At the show he also played guitar on "He Was a Friend of Mine" and joined everyone for a rousing encore of "Only the Lonely."

Above: *In October 1992, an all-star cast celebrated Dylan's thirtieth anniversary as a recording artist at what Neil Young called "Bobfest."*

At this point, Dylan's live performing activities were matched only by his recording. In April he finished *Under the Red Sky* and then spent three weeks in Los Angeles recording another Traveling Wilburys album with Harrison, Lynne, and Petty. Dylan also found time to write a song called "Steel Bars" with bombastic singer Michael Bolton, one of the oddest collaborations Dylan has ever undertaken and one that he apparently instigated. The collaboration received mixed reviews from critics as well as poor sales.

In September, *Under the Red Sky* was released. Despite such an excellent production team, the engineering and mixing talents of Ed Cherney, and musical guests such as George Harrison, Elton John, Jimmy and Stevie Ray Vaughn, Robben Ford, Bruce Hornsby, and Slash from Guns N' Roses, the album was a disappointment for many. Compared to those on *Oh Mercy*, the songs, although well recorded and featuring some music that recalled Dylan's mid-sixties sound, occasionally seemed weak, especially lyrically. The reaction to the album was so discouraging that Dylan decided another album of his songs wouldn't be forthcoming for some time—or ever!

Dylan has often given the impression that even he doesn't know what's next, as was clear in the *Biograph* booklet. "I don't feel like I know what I'm

going to do next week, or not do," he proclaimed. "Mostly I just write songs, make records, and do tours; that takes up most of my time, so I just expect it to go on that way."

In October, Warner Brothers released the second Traveling Wilburys album, oddly entitled *Traveling Wilburys, Volume 3.* Playing the part of Lucky Wilbury on the first album, Dylan this time took the alias Boo. As good as the album was, the fun and spirit of the first album was lacking. With no hit such as "Handle with Care," and Dylan's involvement markedly less than on the first album, somehow the record turned out to be nothing more than just average; considering the talent involved and how great the first was, this album was a disappointment. Perhaps having another artist take the spot vacated by Orbison would have helped. There had at first been rumors that Del Shannon would join the project (Petty was producing him), or that Roger McGuinn would step in. Nonetheless, this was the last anyone would hear of the Traveling Wilburys.

On February 20, 1991, Dylan accepted a Lifetime Achievement Grammy from Jack Nicholson after performing an almost punk version of "Masters of War"—an obvious comment on the unfolding Gulf War. Dylan's acceptance speech was typically oblique, although it was obvious he was delighted to be recognized.

That March, the long anticipated *The Bootleg Series, Volumes 1–3 (Rare & Unreleased), 1961–1991* came out. The three-CD box set contained hotel room recordings, outtakes, live performances, demos, poems, acoustic versions, rehearsals, and alternate takes that were actually mostly early works from the 1960s and 1970s; the eleven tracks from the 1980s were highlighted by the *Infidels* outtake "Blind Willie McTell" and the *Oh Mercy* outtake "Series of Dreams." The title indicated that there would be more to this series; the next

Above left: *Dylan filming in Camden, London, in July 1993 with Dave Stewart of Eurythmics fame.* **Above right:** *After a Prince's Trust concert in England, boxer Frank Bruno, far left, Ron Wood, far right, and Dylan meet Prince Charles.*

Above: *Dylan and Ron Wood, June 1996, at a Prince's Trust benefit concert.*

volumes—rumored to be all live, including the infamous 1966 Royal Albert Hall concert with The Band—were scheduled to come out not long after the first volumes, but as of March 1998, have not been released.

As the Never Ending Tour rolled on, Dylan appeared on David Letterman's tenth-anniversary show on January 18, 1992. With vocal backup supplied by Mavis Staples, Emmylou Harris, Rosanne Cash, Nanci Griffith, and Michele Shocked, Dylan performed "Like a Rolling Stone."

In June Dylan recorded some folk covers on electric guitar with David Bromberg at Acme Recording Studio in Chicago. Throughout the rest of the summer, he recorded an acoustic album of folk and blues songs at his garage studio in Malibu.

In October Dylan began rehearsals for his thirtieth-anniversary concert at Madison Square Garden. He rehearsed at an old soundstage outside Manhattan and then at the Garden. On October 18 the concert took place, with some fine performances of Dylan songs, but there were too many artists who had no connection to Dylan's music other than the fact that they were recording for a Sony-distributed label (of which Columbia is one). Dylan performed "Song to Woody" and "It's Alright Ma, I'm Only Bleeding." He was joined by Neil Young, Eric Clapton, Roger McGuinn, and two of his fellow Wilburys, Tom Petty and George Harrison, on "My Back Pages," and the entire cast helped out on "Knockin' on Heaven's Door." He quietly closed with "Girl from the North Country." Dubbed "Bobfest" by Neil Young, the pay-per-view event was subsequently broadcast over the commercial television airwaves.

On November 3 Dylan released *Good As I Been to You*, a raw, acoustic collection of old folk and blues. His sandpaper-coarse vocals and nimble guitar picking made for authentic blues and folk performances. There are few artists who have any connection to rock music today that could have pulled off a recording so real and spontaneous.

Above: *A couple of Jersey guys, Bruce Springsteen and Frank Sinatra, with Dylan at Sinatra's eightieth birthday party in 1995. Along with Steve Lawrence and Eydie Gorme, Springsteen and Dylan were the only guests invited back to Sinatra's house.*

Dylan kicked off 1993 by playing at the inaugural celebration of President Bill Clinton on January 17. At an event at the Lincoln Memorial, Dylan sang "The Chimes of Freedom." Joining The Band at another party, he performed on several songs, singing and supplying backing guitar.

After the success of *Good As I Been to You*, Dylan headed back to his Malibu home/studio in May to record more acoustic folk and blues. In mid-August, *The Thirtieth Anniversary Concert Celebration* was released as a two-CD set and video that featured highlights of the show. Some of the artists featured include Stevie Wonder, Lou Reed, Johnny Cash, Richie Havens, Neil Young, Eric Clapton, The Band, and George Harrison.

In October, *World Gone Wrong* was released, with Dylan credited as producer. This time, Dylan covered songs originally done by the Mississippi Sheiks ("Blood in My Eyes" and the title cut), Tom Paley of the original New Lost City Ramblers ("Jack-A-Roe"), and Blind Willie McTell ("Broke Down Engine") as well as a song he heard on a Doc Watson record ("Lone Pilgrim") and one he learned from Jerry Garcia ("Two Soldiers"). His delight with the success of the previous album and obvious happiness with this follow-up prompted him to scribe extensive liner notes, which were amusing, informative, and beautifully written, and which sent a message about his touring pace up to that point. In the notes he wrote: "Don't be bewildered by the Never Ending Tour chatter....there was a Never Ending Tour but it ended in '91 with the departure of guitarist G.E. Smith....that one's long gone but there have been many others since then....the Money Never Runs Out Tour (fall of '91), Southern Sympathizer Tour (early '92), Why Do You Look at Me So Strangely Tour (Europe '92), the One Sad Cry of Pity Tour (Australia and West Coast America '92), Principles of Action Tour (Mexico and South America '92), Outburst of Consciousness Tour ('92), Don't Let Your Deal Go Down Tour ('93), and others too many to mention each with their own character and design....to know which was which consult the playlists."

In November Dylan played three nights at Manhattan's Supper Club for a possible *MTV Unplugged* show, for which free tickets were distributed. After the last night, Dylan performed on David Letterman's show.

On August 14, 1994, Dylan played at Woodstock II in Saugerties, New York. Although he opted out of the first festival in 1969, he played a spirited set of electric and acoustic music at the second, which went over very well. The two-CD set of the concert, released later that year on A&M, included Dylan's performance of "Highway 61 Revisited."

The two other significant projects produced by Dylan in 1994 were *Drawn Blank*, a sketchbook of mostly black-and-white pencil drawings from Random House, and *Bob Dylan's Greatest Hits, Volume III*, which included the *Oh Mercy* outtake "Dignity." The book joined *Tarantula* (1971) and *Lyrics:*

1962–1965 (1985, an update of 1973's *Writings and Drawings*) on the list of books Dylan had published. For such a great writer, one would think there would be more published writings from him than this handful of books, occasional liner notes, and other magazine pieces. In the *Biograph* booklet, Dylan mused about other prose ideas: "I started a book awhile back called *Ho Chi Minh in Harlem*. I'd probably like to finish that. Maybe write stories the way Kerouac did, about some of the people I know and knew, change the names."

After deciding not to release the Supper Club recordings and film, Dylan began rehearsing for an *MTV Unplugged* taping. On November 17 and 18 he performed for MTV's cameras at Sony Music Studios in Manhattan; the results were put together by MTV and subsequently released as an album and video in April 1995.

In February 1995 Dylan entered the interactive age with the *Highway 61 Interactive* CD-ROM, which included plenty of videos, unreleased music, and a point-and-click tour of the life and music of Bob Dylan. There is an enhanced CD, in both MAC and Windows formats, of his third volume of greatest hits that also contains multimedia presentations of rarities. Dylan continued his breakneck touring pace while in March his *World Gone Wrong* album won a Grammy in the Traditional Folk category. Also in March his cover of the Doc Pomus song "Boogie Woogie Country Girl," which was recorded in New Orleans, came out on *Till the Night Is Gone: A Tribute to Doc Pomus*.

Released in April, the *MTV Unplugged* special was an unquestionable success. The ecstatic audience was treated to such Dylan classics as "All Along the

Above: *Two holy men: Dylan and the Pope.*

Watchtower," "The Times They Are A-Changin'," "Rainy Day Women #12 & 35," "Knockin' on Heaven's Door," and "Like a Rolling Stone." The video and CD, in fact, contain five songs that were not on the original MTV broadcast, including a 1963 composition, "John Brown," that had not previously been captured on any video or audio recording. Another song that appears on the video, "Love Minus Zero/No Limit," is not on the CD.

Dylan's backing band was exceptional. Organist Brendan O'Brien appeared very involved in the musical direction and arrangements, while Winston Watson gave Dylan a crisp, fresh drum attack. Frontman John Jackson on guitar and stand-up bassist Tony Garnier provided superb support. The real star of the band, though, was Bucky Baxter on dobro and other instruments. Throughout most of the 1990s, Dylan's more stripped down groups have had a rough edge. This has kept Dylan's live shows invigorated, but has also made many songs rushed and messy, and has not always given Dylan the time or musical space he needs to sing his songs properly. Baxter's playing brought a sweeter, country feel to the proceedings that allowed Dylan to articulate his vocals, bring out different vocal shadings, and put more of an emphasis on songs from his repertoire that were more melodic. There were flashes of Dylan almost smiling during the taping and at the end he took off his shades, acknowledged the audience's obvious unanimous approval, shared smiles and a brief laugh with Garnier, and seemed relieved that the whole thing was over and had gone off well. Coming after the release of his two acoustic outings and representing the latest live document of Dylan's music, the show put Dylan at a winning musical crossroads once again.

In September Dylan, along with a who's who of rock—past, present, and future—played at the grand opening of the Rock and Roll Hall of Fame in Cleveland, Ohio. He performed five songs and was joined by Bruce Springsteen for "Forever Young." Continuing a year of nonstop activity, Dylan performed at Frank Sinatra's eightieth-birthday tribute at the Shrine Auditorium in Los Angeles. He wanted to perform "That's Life," but in a testament to Sinatra's endless knowledge of music, he obliged Sinatra by performing his own "Restless Farewell." After the taping, a few select guests were invited back to Sinatra's house: the opening act, Steve Lawrence and Edie Gorme, Springsteen, and Dylan.

That December, Dylan played another set of shows that entered rock history on the Paradise Lost Tour. His opening act for all the shows was Patti Smith. These shows were not about Dylan; rather, they were a vehicle for Smith to return to performing after years away from the stage. As the tour progressed, Smith joined Dylan on stage, and reports of Dylan's complete delight at singing with Smith were made clear by the mile-wide smile on his face.

In January 1996 Dylan recorded "Ring of Fire" for the film *Feeling Minnesota.* That same month he received three Grammy nominations for his

MTV Unplugged album. In September his performance of "All Along the Watchtower" was released on the double CD *The Concert for the Rock and Roll Hall of Fame.* While Dylan's artistic output in 1996 was mostly comprised of playing live with his excellent backing band, 1997 was a year of recording focus. In 1998, Dylan won three Grammys for Album of the Year and Contemporary Folk Album of the Year for *Time Out of Mind,* and Male Rock Performance for "Cold Irons Bound." His son Jakob's band, The Wallflowers, won for Best Rock Performance by a Duo or Group with Vocal and Best Rock Song for "One Headlight."

Coda

The story of Bob Dylan does not end here. For one thing, it appears that there is much more that Dylan wants to do. Also, there are many who want to honor Dylan for his contributions to music, culture and history. 1997 proved that Dylan's creative drive is still burning. There was, however, a period in the late spring and early summer when Dylan's mortality was clearly evident.

On May 25th, a day after his 56th birthday, precipitated by chest pains, Dylan entered the hospital suffering from pericarditis, a swelling of the heart sac, brought on by a fungal infection called histoplasmosis. Initially a very serious illness, it caused Dylan to cancel his European tour; however, he quickly bounced back and went ahead with his U. S. tour. If the infection had attacked an organ other than his heart it apparently wouldn't have been life-threatening. It did keep him off his feet for six weeks, during which time he had to take medication three times a day. As serious as things were, when Dylan had fully recuperated, he joked in a press release, "I really thought I'd be seeing Elvis

soon," putting to rest forever the myth that Dylan has no sense of humor.

As his U.S. tour commenced, the first release on Dylan's new record label, Egyptian Records, came out. It was called *The Songs Of Jimmie Rodgers, A Tribute*. Along with Dylan's reading of "My Blue Eyed Jane," the album included Jerry Garcia's last recording, "Blue Yodel # 9," which also featured David Grisman and John Kahn. Other artists that contributed were Bono, Willie Nelson, and Van Morrison, among many others.

Proving that Dylan's newer songs still resonate with today's musical artists, on *Billy Joel's Greatest Hits Volume III*, released in August, there was an impassioned cover of the 1997 Dylan song, "To Make You Feel My Love," produced by Peter Asher, that was easily one of Joel's best recordings in years.

With Dylan's tour under way, an old friend, freed on probation from a Japanese jail on drug charges, popped up: Rick Danko of The Band joined Dylan at The Oakdale in Wallingford, Connecticut, on August 18th, and they performed "This Wheel's On Fire," a song they wrote together that appeared on The Band's debut, *Music From Big Pink*, and "I Shall Be Released," Dylan's composition, which also appeared on *Big Pink*.

A month prior to the release of his new album, entitled *Time Out Of Mind*, word on the Dylan grapevine was that he would perform for Pope John Paul II on September 27th at the World Eucharistic Congress in Bologna, Italy, further illustrating Dylan's stature as an artist and the respect he commands from so many segments of society.

Only weeks before the release of his new album in September, more Dylan news was circulating. A reissue of *Biograph*, which contained slightly incorrect mixes of a few songs, was swiftly recalled by Columbia Records, making it an instant collector's item. There was also word that Dylan would be honored at the twentieth annual John F. Kennedy Center awards at the White House on December 7th of 1997. The lifetime achievement award would be presented by President Bill Clinton and a subsequent two-hour telecast would be taped and broadcast on the CBS television network.

The biggest news, though, for Dylan fans was the release on September 30th of *Time Out Of Mind*. His first full album of all new songs since 1990's *Under The Red Sky*, on it Dylan teamed up again with Daniel Lanois, who produced the brilliant *Oh Mercy*, the album prior to *Under The Red Sky*. Clearly Lanois knows exactly how to get the best out of Dylan. *Time Out Of Mind* is a monumental achievement. It may, in fact, be the best album Dylan has done since 1975's *Blood On The Tracks*, and it shares some of the same themes that Dylan explored on that album.

Time Out Of Mind is a very dark and moody album. It doesn't have the weighty, cinematic feel of *Oh Mercy*, but it does occasionally have the same murky, atmospheric musical undertow. It has a distinctive blues feel. The centerpiece of the album is the sixteen-minute-long "Highlands," a meditation on lost love and living in these last days of the millennium. Written and recorded long before Dylan's illness, the album reflects the thoughts of an artist about his own mortality. There has perhaps never been another album recorded by a rock artist on which the artist has so directly looked at his own mortality, and in light of Dylan's May illness, it can be seen as almost eerily prophetic.

More than anything else, though, the album's strength shows that Dylan has a lot more music ahead of him. The songwriting, singing, and playing are

Above: *Dylan performing at the 1996 Prince's Trust concert in Hyde Park England.*

some of the best he has ever done. The mixing of musical styles and Dylan's ability to stretch out as a songwriter are nothing short of remarkable. It's obvious that there are many more great songs to be written by him. Also, Dylan again has found the perfect cast to support him musically, as evidenced by pianist Jim Dickinson, organist Augie Myers, and blues guitarist Duke Robillard guesting, with near-perfect results.

Bob Dylan's future is as uncertain as any man's. It looks like the stage is the place he is most comfortable, however. The clearest insight that could be drawn from his music that best points toward his future would come from the lines in "Tangled Up In Blue" from his *Blood On The Tracks* album: "...me, I'm still on the road/Headin' for another joint/We always did feel the same/We just saw it from a different point of view/Tangled up in blue."

Above: *Dylan at the Phoenix Festival.*

Discography

This discography represents the original releases of all of Bob Dylan's U.S. albums, with each original record label noted.

Bob Dylan. March 1962, Columbia.

The Freewheelin' Bob Dylan. May 1963, Columbia.

The Times They Are A-Changin'. January 1964, Columbia.

Another Side of Bob Dylan. August 1964, Columbia.

Bringing It All Back Home. March 1965, Columbia.

Highway 61 Revisited. August 1965, Columbia.

Blonde on Blonde. May 1966, Columbia.

Bob Dylan's Greatest Hits. March 1967, Columbia.

John Wesley Harding. December 1967, Columbia.

Nashville Skyline. April 1969, Columbia.

Self Portrait. June 1970, Columbia.

New Morning. October 1970, Columbia.

Bob Dylan's Greatest Hits, Volume II. November 1971, Columbia.

Pat Garrett & Billy the Kid soundtrack. July 1973, Columbia.

Dylan. November 1973, Columbia.

Planet Waves. January 1974, Asylum.

Before the Flood. June 1974, Asylum.

Blood on the Tracks. January 1975, Columbia.

The Basement Tapes. June 1975, Columbia.

Desire. January 1976, Columbia.

Hard Rain. September 1976, Columbia.

Street Legal. June 1978, Columbia.

At Budokan. July 1978, Columbia.

Slow Train Coming. August 1979, Columbia.

Saved. June 1980, Columbia.

Shot of Love. August 1981, Columbia.

Infidels. November 1983, Columbia.

Real Live. December 1984, Columbia.

Empire Burlesque. June 1985, Columbia.

Biograph. October 1985, Columbia.

Knocked Out Loaded. August 1986, Columbia.

Hearts of Fire soundtrack, three songs. October 1987, Columbia.

Down in the Groove. May 1988, Columbia.

Folkways: A Vision Shared. August 1988, Columbia.

Traveling Wilburys, Volume 1. October 1988, Warner Brothers.

Dylan & the Dead. February 1989, Columbia.

Oh Mercy. September 1989, Columbia.

Under the Red Sky. September 1990, Columbia.

Traveling Wilburys, Volume 3. October 1990, Warner Brothers.

The Bootleg Series, Volumes 1–3 (Rare & Unreleased), 1961–1991. March 1991, Columbia.

Good As I Been to You. October 1992, Columbia.

The Thirtieth Anniversary Concert Celebration. August 1993, Columbia.

World Gone Wrong. October 1993, Columbia.

Bob Dylan's Greatest Hits, Volume III. November 1994, Columbia.

MTV Unplugged. April 1995, Columbia.

Time Out of Mind. September 1997, Columbia.

Other recordings with significant contributions by Bob Dylan:

The Concert for Bangladesh. Various artists. January 1972, Apple.

The Last Waltz. The Band and various artists. April 1978, Warner Brothers.

Recordings by other artists that include material mostly or completely written by Bob Dylan:

Any Day Now. Joan Baez. 1968, Vanguard.

Sings Beatles and Dylan (Old & New Together & Apart). Richie Havens. 1987, Rykodisc.

Just Like a Woman (Judy Collins Sings Dylan). Judy Collins. 1993, Geffen.

Red on Blonde. Tim O'Brien. 1996, Sugar Hill.

Theatrical films, television films, television shows, and videos in which Bob Dylan had a principal or major theatrical or performing role (asterisk indicates available on video):

Backtrack

The Concert for Bangladesh*

Don't Look Back*

Eat the Document

Hard Rain (television special)

Hard to Handle* (HBO special)

Hearts of Fire* (video only—no U.S. theatrical release)

The Last Waltz*

MTV Unplugged*

Pat Garrett & Billy the Kid*

Renaldo & Clara

Suggested Reading

The books included here are by no means all the books about Bob Dylan, or all the information about him, the artists that are significant to his works, or the times he has lived in. This list reflects books from the author's library that were most pertinent to the research for this biography.

Books by Bob Dylan:

Drawn Blank. New York: Random House, 1994.

Lyrics: 1962–1985. (an update of *Writings and Drawings*). New York: Knopf, 1985.

Tarantula. New York: Macmillan, 1971.

Writings and Drawings. New York: Knopf, 1973.

Books about Bob Dylan:

Bauldie, John, ed. *Wanted Man: In Search of Bob Dylan*. Secaucus: Citadel, 1991.

Cott, Jonathan. *Dylan*. New York: Rolling Stone Press/Doubleday, 1984.

Dowley, Tim, and Barry Dunnage, eds. *From a Hard Rain to a Slow Train*. New York: Omnibus Press, 1982.

Heylin, Clinton. *Bob Dylan: Behind the Shades*. New York: Summit Books, 1991.

———. *A Life in Stolen Moments*. New York: Schirmer Books, 1996.

———. *The Recording Sessions*. New York: St. Martin's Press, 1995.

Humphries, Patrick, and John Bauldie. *Absolutely Dylan*. New York: Viking Studio Books, 1991.

Kramer, Daniel. *Bob Dylan*. Secaucus: Citadel, 1991.

Marcus, Greil. *Invisible Republic*. New York: Henry Holt, 1997.

Riley, Tim. *Hard Rain*. New York: Knopf, 1992.

Rowley, Chris. *Blood on the Tracks*. New York: Proteus, 1984.

Scaduto, Anthony. *Bob Dylan*. New York: Signet, 1973.

Shelton, Robert. *No Direction Home*. New York: William Morrow, 1986.

Shepard, Sam. *Rolling Thunder Logbook*. New York: Viking Press, 1977.

Spitz, Bob. *Dylan*. New York: McGraw-Hill, 1989.

Thompson, Elizabeth, and David Gutman, eds. *The Dylan Companion*. New York: Delta, 1990.

Williams, Christine. *Bob Dylan: In His Own Words*. New York: Omnibus Press, 1993.

Williams, Paul. *Performing Artist: The Music of Bob Dylan*. Novato: Underwood-Miller, 1990.

Williams, Richard. *Dylan: A Man Called Alias*. New York: Henry Holt, 1992.

Additional books about music, the business of music, and related matters:

Baez, Joan. *And a Voice to Sing With*. New York: Summit Books, 1987.

Eliot, Marc. *Death of a Rebel: A Biography of Phil Ochs*. Danbury: Franklin Watts, 1989.

Fornatale, Pete. *The Story of Rock 'n' Roll*. New York: William Morrow, 1987.

Goodman, Fred. *The Mansion on the Hill*. New York: Times Books, 1997.

Graham, Bill, and Robert Greenfield. *Bill Graham Presents*. New York: Doubleday, 1992.

Guthrie, Woody. *Bound for Glory*. New York: Dutton, 1943.

Hammond, John, and Irving Townsend. *John Hammond on Record*. New York: Ridge Press, 1977.

Harris, Craig. *The New Folk Music*. Crown Point: White Cliffs Media, 1991.

Helm, Levon, and Stephen Davis. *This Wheel's on Fire*. New York: William Morrow, 1993.

Hoskyns, Barney. *The Band and America*. New York: Hyperion, 1993.

Klein, Joe. *Woody Guthrie: A Life*. New York: Ballantine, 1980.

Landy, Elliot. *Woodstock Vision*. New York: Continuum, 1994.

Marcus, Greil. *Mystery Train*. New York: Dutton, 1982.

Myrus, Donald. *Ballads, Blues and the Big Beat*. New York: Macmillan, 1966.

Nolan, A.M. *Rock 'n' Roll Road Trip*. New York: Pharos Books, 1992.

Palmer, Robert. *Deep Blues*. New York: Viking Press, 1981.

Peellaert, Guy, and Nik Cohn. *Rock Dreams*. Hamburg: Rogner & Bernhard, 1982.

Perry, Tim, and Ed Glinert. *Rock & Roll Traveler USA*. New York: Fodor's, 1996.

Sarlin, Bob. *Turn It Up! (I Can't Hear the Words)*. New York: Simon & Schuster, 1973.

Schmidt, Eric, and Jim Rooney. *Baby Let Me Follow You Down*. Amherst: University of Massachusetts Press, 1994.

Woliver, Robbie. *Bringing It All Back Home*. New York: Pantheon, 1986.

Books on media:

Crenshaw, Marshall. *Hollywood Rock*. New York: HarperCollins, 1994.

Fornatale, Peter, and Joshua Mills. *Radio in the Television Age*. New York: Overlook Press, 1980.

Sandahl, Linda. *Rock Films*. New York: Facts on File, 1987.

Books on related history and culture:

Branch, Taylor. *Parting the Waters: America in the King Years, 1954–1963*. New York: Simon & Schuster, 1988.

Caute, David. *The Year of the Barricades: A Journey Through 1968*. New York: Harper & Row, 1968.

Charters, Ann. *Kerouac: A Biography*. San Francisco: Straight Arrow Books, 1973.

———. *The Portable Beat Reader*. New York: Viking/Penguin, 1992.

Hayden, Tom. *Reunion*. New York: Random House, 1988.

McClure, Michael. *Scratching the Beat Surface*. San Francisco: North Point Press, 1982.

McDarrah, Fred, and Gloria McDarrah. *Beat Generation: Glory Days in Greenwich Village*. New York: Schirmer Books, 1996.

Miles, Barry. *Ginsberg: A Biography*. New York: Simon & Schuster, 1989.

Stein, Jean, and George Plimpton, eds. *Edie: An American Biography*. New York: Knopf, 1982.

Related fiction:

Farina, Richard. *Been Down So Long It Looks Like Up to Me*. New York: Random House, 1966.

Kerouac, Jack. *On the Road*. New York: Viking Press, 1957.

Morton, Brian. *The Dylanist*. New York: HarperCollins, 1991.

Salinger, J.D. *The Catcher in the Rye*. Boston: Little, Brown, 1951.

Photography Credits

Index